a guide to 21st century singapore architecture

First published in 2012

Editor: Patrick Bingham-Hall
Graphic design : Stephen Smedley, Tonto Design
Design production : Pesaro Publishing and Ayeemm Cabales

Pesaro Publishing
14 Robinson Road #13-00
Far East Finance Building
Singapore 048545

Pesaro Publishing
PO Box 74
Balmain NSW 2041
Sydney, Australia

www.pesaropublishing.com

National Library Board, Singapore Cataloguing-in-Publication Data

Bingham-Hall, Patrick.

A guide to 21st century Singapore architecture / author & photographer,
Patrick Bingham-Hall. – Singapore : Pesaro Pub., 2012 .

p. cm.

Includes index.

ISBN : 978-981-4428-00-2

1. Architecture – Singapore – History – 21st century. I. Title.

NA1530.S5

720.95957 -- dc23 OCN796386193

ISBN 978-981-4428-00-2

Printed by Imago

a guide to 21st century singapore architecture

text and photography by
patrick bingham-hall

pesaro publishing

contents

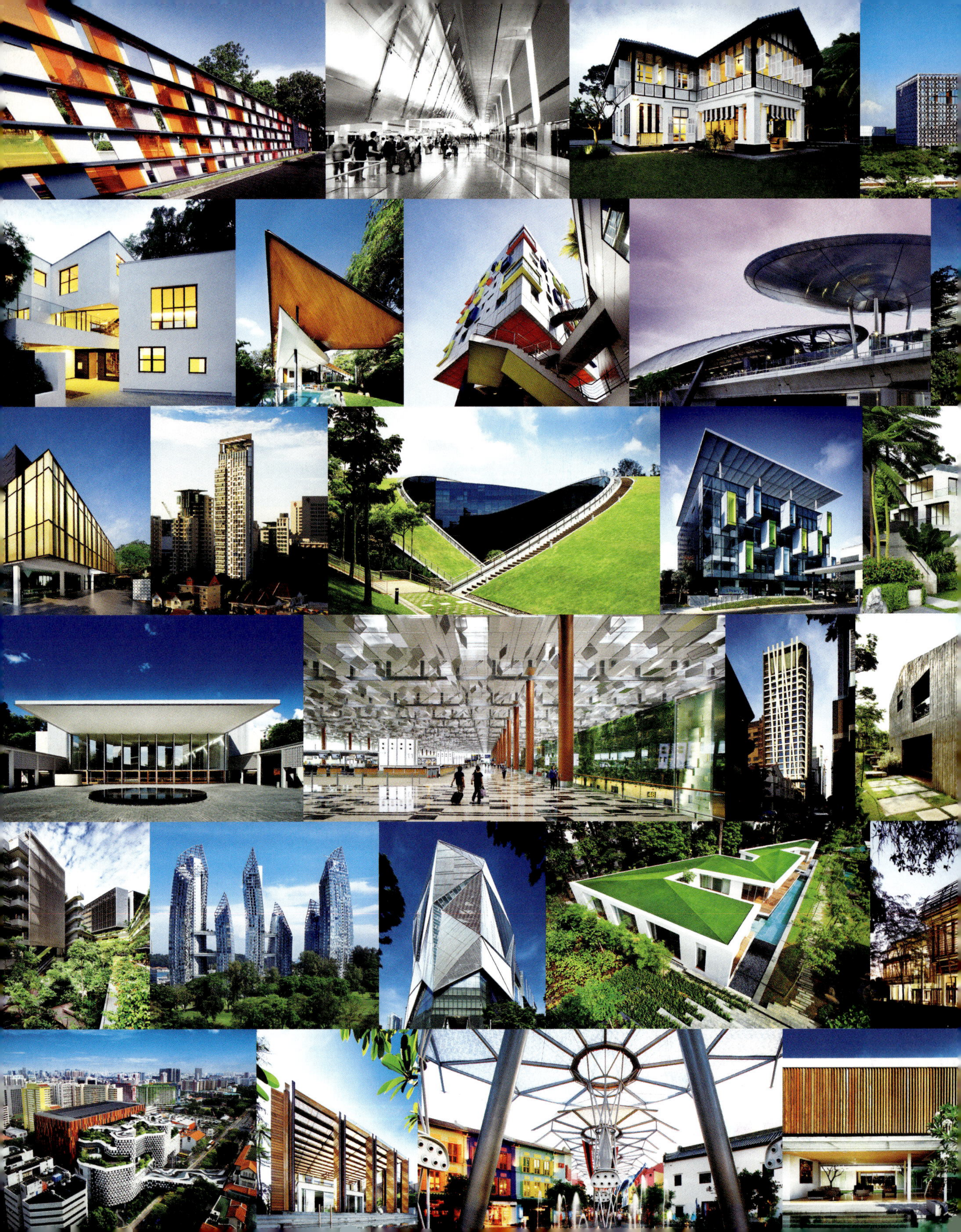

CROWNE PLAZA
National Museum of Singapore

new venice, new amsterdam, new new york

They believed that by dazzling their visitors with the city's architecture and pomp they could create an atmosphere of impregnability and security, and so disguise their lack of territory and land defences.[1]

As a litmus test of 21st century global architectural activity and intent, Singapore cannot be improved upon. Unlike the cities of China or the Middle East, it has not emerged as a garden of iconic delights after decades of obscurity, and unlike the cities of the Old World, it has not been hit by a savage economic downturn. At the very heart of a momentous geo-political swing – at the junction between East and West, and Old and New– Singapore currently occupies a unique position: it is an affluent city, it is one of the world's largest ports and financial centres, and it requires infrastructure and new buildings (lots of them) for which it is prepared to pay, and from which it demands both usefulness and aesthetic satisfaction. Singapore is a new New York, and its architecture and city planning reflect a new 21st century reality.

The architecture of cities has always defined a civilisation, and the buildings of the great cities are the monuments of our culture as, to paraphrase John Ruskin, the art (and the architecture) is more trustworthy to the eyes of a historian than the books of the words and the deeds. To truly understand the cultures of the past, one must visit those great cities – Rome, Florence, Paris, London, even New York – which now exist (in part) as museums of that past. What set those cities apart, at a certain point in time, was the excess of architecture: the sheer amount of construction that occurred whilst the city and its civilisation (however that may have been defined) was thriving at a higher level and a greater speed than its contemporaries. As to how 21st century Singapore will eventually be inscribed upon the history of human civilisation – as another Venice, another Bruges, another Amsterdam, or as another Buenos Aires – has yet to be played out, but so much has been designed and built by so many in the last decade that the city has become, for

1 J.G. Links, *Canaletto*, Phaidon Press, London, 2nd edition, 1994. p8. These lines are taken from *Age of Illusion*, the opening chapter of the acknowledged standard work on the 18th century Venetian master painter, Canaletto. Comparisons between 18th century Venice and 21st century Singapore are fanciful, as the Venetian city-state was then in decline after 1100 years of 'punching above its weight', whilst contemporary Singapore is still on the rise after forty years of 'over-achievement'. Yet the role of architecture as a symbol of presumed power and wealth (and its value as a tourist attraction) is integral to the continued sustenance of a city-state.

better or worse, a monument – if not the monument – to its times. An acknowledgment of this circumstance will inevitably overwhelm the assessment of individual architects and their buildings, as the city can only really be viewed as a collective enterprise: much like the New York of the mid-20th century, where criticism of and praise for certain buildings is immediately contextualised by the impact of the architecture and what it represented. Singapore has had more cranes on the skyline than other globally significant city for ten years now: the city is having its time in the early 21st century sun, and does not look like giving up that privilege in the foreseeable future.[2]

If the architecture of a great city is the mark of a civilisation's culture, so too will it reflect the social issues of the age. The civilisation that contemporary Singapore may be taken to represent is both regional and global, which is a logical extension of the city's historical role – the word '*entrepôt*' was seemingly invented for Singapore – and as globalisation gradually morphs into Asianisation, the ability of the city-state to confront and to solve endemic problems will have a profound impact. Singapore is at the Southeast Asian epicentre of the 21st century predicaments of global warming and urban overcrowding, so the requirement to be pro-active is now taken to be unavoidable. The problems will probably be solved, or at least remediated, by architecture, infrastructure and urban planning, which is an area where Singapore is obliged to take the lead: it is the only First World country in tropical Asia, and it operates at a level of seamless inter-connectivity with other technologically advanced nations. For example, as part of the island-wide water management scheme, a rudimentary storm-water canal and an under-used stretch of grassed land between the suburbs of Bishan and Ang Mo Kio were transformed into a contemporary version of the 19th century picturesque urban park. Atelier Dreiseitl, the landscape architects and hydrological consultants, are German, and Singapore (through the Public Utilities Board) paid for the project because it considered flood control and water self-sufficiency to be necessary. The scheme can be seen as a regional prototype, as many of Singapore's neighbours – Bangkok, Dhaka, Jakarta – are forever threatened by floodwaters, as can many other environmental and (non CBD) urban planning initiatives.

Architecture itself (and the planning of the inner-city to which much of it responds) has been a lot less sure-footed and communally persuasive, and this may well be due to an inherent weakness in late 20th century architectural discourse, which led to an abrogation

2 In 2010, the IMF stated that Singapore (the nation) had the world's third highest per capita GDP. The Global Power City Index 2011, released by the Institute for Urban Strategies at The Mori Memorial Foundation in Japan, ranked Singapore as the world's fifth most powerful city, and predicted that it will overtake Tokyo as number four within seven years, and other such studies over the last decade have routinely placed Singapore in the world's top ten most significant cities. 2011 data ranks Singapore as the world's second busiest port and fourth busiest financial centre. When Singapore achieved independence in 1965, it was little more than a run-down resource-free remnant of a dismantled empire.

Bishan – Ang Mo Kio Park (2012), Atelier Dreiseitl

of any responsibility beyond that of individual expression within a self-referential global architectural community. As the Singaporean economy (and its concomitant self-confidence) grew rapidly in the 1970s, the decision was made by the ruthlessly ambitious government to erect a cityscape that would reflect the new status of the city, and, as with so many other projects at the time, the prevailing opinion was that only international consultants would have the expertise (and, in the case of architecture, the cachet) to deliver the pre-requisite. But, although some of the first buildings were quite impressive, it would appear that over the longer term, the Singaporeans were sold a pup, and one which was just not suited to tropical Asia. Very few landmark buildings had anything to offer as prototypes for large-scale (or indeed small-scale) tropical architecture, and to be quite frank, not many appeared to be anything other than what the architects would have erected in their hometowns in Europe, the United States and Japan. With a few exceptions, Singapore was let down by the failure of a generation of architects to engage with anything that lay outside esoteric discussions within a global design compound: form-making and the implementation of a certain style, or representation, appear to have been more compelling than a specific solution to an endemic problem. To be fair, the obligation to environmental sustainability did not gain credence until the early 1990s, but the architecture had, nonetheless, only paid occasional heed – formal, aesthetic or material – to its location. The reaction of the ensuing generation of local and international architects to that evasion of commitment tells much of the story of the last ten years: not all of it has been edifying, as many international architects refuse to jettison any of that which they know so well (and in doing so they are possibly reassuring a certain clientele), but several Singaporeans are sowing appropriate and sustainable seeds.

We May Never See Their Like Again… (A Short History of Singapore Architecture)

Upon the signing of a treaty between Sir Stamford Raffles of the British East India Company and the Temenggong Abdul Rahman on February 6, 1819, the British founded modern Singapore – on an island occupied by approximately one thousand inhabitants – with the express intention of countering the Dutch control of the Malacca Straits shipping route and a desire to set up a free port (as opposed to those of the Dutch). Within four years, five thousand new settlers – mostly locally born Chinese (Peranakans) and Indians – had decamped from

I am astonished to see how markedly our world is changing. A new world is being created, the old world destroyed. The very jungle becomes a settled district while elsewhere a settlement reverts to jungle.[3]

Munshi Abdullah (early 1840s)

Arab Street

Melaka, which had been returned to the Dutch by the British in 1818, and by 1869 the population had reached 100,000, with something like half a million ships passing through the port each year. Raffles, who actually spent very little time in Singapore, had established a town plan in 1822 that allocated separate precincts for the various racial communities, and most pertinently, he implemented a rectangular grid of streets with frontages that took the climate into account: rows of shophouses incorporated street-level arcades, known as five-foot-ways, which provided continuous shaded and sheltered circulation throughout the settlement. The shophouses themselves were rather cramped and gloomy, but they were ventilated by internal light-wells that were open to the elements.

After the opening of the Suez Canal in 1869, the population grew to 200,000 by the turn of the century, and an architecture of affluence was to sprout in the more pleasurable out-of-town locations. Wealthy residents, known as *towkays*, and the colonial administrators built substantial bungalows that indulged in the tropical landscape and the lifestyle that it offered (some of them remain, most notably the Black & White Houses of the 1920s). Another form of semi-rural (or suburban) housing, which was often built as a villa near the coast, derived from the elevated and relatively lightweight *kampung* house, as can still be seen throughout the Malay Peninsula. Very

3 Munshi Abdullah, *Hikiyat Abdullah*, pp.39-52. As quoted in Mark R. Frost and Yu-Mei Balasingamchow, *Singapore: A Biography*, Editions Didier Millet, Singapore, 2009. p75. Completed in the early 1840s, the *Hikiyat Abdullah* (The Story of Abdullah) is described by Frost and Balasingamchow as "... the most comprehensive eyewitness account of early 19th century Singapore by a non-European." They also note that "... while Abdullah was definitely an advocate of any of the advances brought to the region by Europeans, on more than one occasion the *Hikiyat's* pages are tinged by the author's regret at the endlessly changing present that he lived in."

few of these villas remain *in situ*, as the house component is no longer commensurate with the real estate value of its land. In a style referred to as 'Straits Chinese', the shophouses of the 1920s and 1930s featured ornate and colourfully crafted façades, which bestowed Singapore with an idiosyncratic – and decidedly non-architectural – personality that continues to subvert higher-minded visions of national identity. This period also saw the establishment of formal architectural practices in the colony, which – somewhat predictably – specialised in stiff and stolid Beaux-Arts public buildings without a sniff of tropical exotica.

Modernism made an appearance in the 1930s, and the architecture looked surprisingly tropical in the hands of some local architects: an elegant lightweight modernist style evolved, which used slender projecting eaves, large picture windows and ventilated circulation routes over many levels. The Chee Guan Chiang House (1938, by Ho Kwong Yew) was a beautifully proportioned three-storey villa with shaded semi-circular balconies standing in its own grounds at the eastern end of Grange Road (and so it remains, derelict, at the time of writing). This incipient localised modernism was co-opted by the Singapore Improvement Trust (SIT), most memorably in the designs for the Tiong Bahru Housing Estate (1936-1954), which survives intact – and lovingly preserved – as a very special set-piece of public housing that has, quite frankly, never been improved upon as a prototype for tropical mass-housing. And it was a much-copied and much-modified prototype, as the SIT morphed into the HDB (Housing and Development Board) in 1960. The first of Singapore's new townships was built at Queenstown in the early 1970s, with strikingly graphic blocks of apartments – clearly influenced by the plastic expressionism of Hans Scharoun – that provided ventilation and protection from the sun and rain. Subsequent HDB projects were to slowly sink into relative architectural mediocrity, but the spirit of the local modernists was to triumph, inevitably and almost heroically, with a flush of buildings designed in the 1960s and early 1970s whose optimistic fervour reflected the radical reshaping of the nation's identity and destiny after the British relinquished power in 1959.

Chee Guan Chiang House

Tiong Bahru Housing Estate

The seminal early buildings of this 'semi-heroic' period have either been demolished (the National Theatre, by Alfred Wong, 1963) or altered beyond all redemption (NTUC Conference Hall, by Malayan Architects Co-Partnership, 1965), but a handful of stunningly uncompromising, nay monumental structures remain (although threatened with ignominious vapourisation whenever soul-less rapacity gets up a head of steam). The Peoples Park Complex (1973, by Design Partnership) – a massive vertical slab sitting atop an equally massive podium – and the Woh Hup Complex (1974, also by Design Partnership, and now known as the Golden Mile Complex) – with a gigantic stepped section – appeared, and still appear, to be way ahead of their time. The Pearl Bank Apartments (1976, by Archurban) and the Futura Apartments (1976, by Timothy Seow) were equally audacious, as was the Jurong Town Hall (1974, by Architects Team 3), which resembled some kind of hugely over-scaled inhabitable ship or dirigible: a fantastic futurist vision that actually got built (with a tip of the hat to Archigram). Most of these projects were built as the government, through the URA (Urban Redevelopment Authority), released land for sale as part of its urban renewal strategy, but the next round of land sales, in the mid 1970s, opened the door to foreign architects, and the hot-house atmosphere that had produced such inimitable structures (which, incidentally, were conspicuously attuned to local climatic conditions) was wiped out: we may never see their like again.

Pearl Bank Apartments

Jurong Town Hall

The foreign invasion was a rout: local architects were quickly marginalised as bit players and suburban polemicists, or glorified pencil-holders for the visitors. Viewed in one way (geo-politically?), the results were unequivocally successful, as Singapore rapidly established itself as a corporate centre and tourist destination that conformed to the global 'same same' environment, whilst quietly shedding local colour and eccentricity. And that, of course, was the main game: First World status in record time, for which indisputably First World architecture by First World architects would be required. The earliest tower designed by a foreign architect, I.M. Pei's OCBC Centre (1976), was possibly the best of them all, and its form and assertiveness looked like an appropriate continuation of the proud monumentality only recently displayed by the displaced locals. No other Singaporean work by an international architect for the next twenty-five years is really worthy of attention, apart from another project by I.M. Pei – an especially sleek pair of knife-edged towers known as The Gateway (1991) – and two locally influential buildings by Paul Rudolph: The Colonnade (1985) and The Concourse (1994). The Colonnade, an upmarket condominium, comprised twenty-eight floors of modular cubes stacked as a honeycomb upon cylindrical columns, whilst the mixed-use Concourse had rows of inwardly inclined windows arrayed beneath projecting floor plates on an octagonal plan. Both of Rudolph's structures could be read as clearly expressed diagrams for protection from heat and rain. Viewed in another way – in terms of local aspiration – the foreign invasion was a double-edged sword: architecture was now firmly part of the process that had economically transformed Singapore, so there was work to be had and experience to be gained, but only very rarely was a significant project to be designed – without advice or hindrance – by local architects.

Until the late 1990s and the aftermath of the Southeast Asian financial crisis, trends in local architecture fluttered to and fro, as those practitioners who could not deign to play a role as a supporting actor picked up work wherever they could: community centres, schools, health facilities and private house design. The fluctuations in style stemmed from a lack of confidence and direction, as the more that local architects spoke of the need for an architectural identity, the more that identity was being determined by their government and multi-national developers. A small budget community centre or secondary school could never be emblematic of Singapore, no matter how the architects attempted to romanticise their polemic, but as the foreign architects were conspicuously failing in their endeavours to supply Singapore with an architectural identity (apart from that of a corporate tidy town), the local architects had a point. Some of them flirted with post-modernism, but it looked incongruous in Singapore (the colours faded rapidly and the references were too obscure), whilst others – notably Tay Kheng Soon – continued to adapt modernist principles to a tropical context. Tay, along with William Lim, had been a leading figure in Design Partnership, which had designed many of the bravura early 1970s schemes, but their subsequent projects never recaptured that spirit of the times: a generation of architects devoted themselves to defining a local architecture, but they were somehow distancing themselves from what had become the main game in a relentlessly ambitious environment.

Truly Tropical Architecture

The chronology of buildings featured in this book begins in the year 2000, as (irrespective of any millennial portents) that was the year that Singapore emerged from the black hole of the 1997 Southeast Asian economic crisis and building activity resumed apace. The construction rate has not slackened since (there was not even a momentary blip on building sites in 1998), and the cityscape has been transformed in every way. Twelve years ago, the Singapore skyline looked like that of a large American provincial city and the scale of its surrounding urban network was similar to any large Asian city, but by 2012, the skyline – which extends well beyond the CBD – is that of a global *über* city, and the scale and density of the urban mass has followed accordingly.

When large-scale construction regained momentum, three significant public projects – the Esplanade Theatres on the Bay, the Supreme Court, and the National Library – got underway in the Civic District north of the Singapore River. These three projects, not entirely coincidentally, evinced something other than corporate blandness and a gratuitous transportation of cold-climate architecture. The original scheme for the Esplanade Theatres had endured much controversy when unveiled to the public in 1994, as the twin forms of the theatres were criticised for being 'too Western and not tropical enough'. These objections were duly remediated by DP Architects (the local firm who had partnered London-based Michael Wilford on the initial design) and the resulting structures were deemed sufficiently Singaporean: a process that marked quite a change in local attitude. The National Library (by Ken Yeang) and the Supreme Court (by Norman Foster) were both clever tropically-

National Library (2005), T.R. Hamzah and Yeang with DP Architects

inflected buildings, designed by architects who have made their commitment to sustainability and contextual awareness abundantly clear. So by 2005, Singapore had a triptych of modern buildings in its public precinct that enhanced the ideals of civic decorum, and established a notion of place and identity that could actually be construed as local.

The 1990s had seen a dwindling of enthusiasm on the part of all involved with Singapore architecture: the foreign architects weren't really giving it their best shot, as evidenced by the mind-numbingly tedious office blocks and hotels that comprised the Suntec City and Marina Centre developments; a generation or two of local architects had lost the fire in their bellies; and the governmental authorities appeared unsure of which direction to take. The financial crisis was possibly something of a blessing in disguise, as the treadmill stopped for a while, and when it began again, there were some new players with new priorities. Sustainability was now part of the architectural lexicon, and when coupled with notions of appropriate tropical architecture, the attitude of 'anything can be built anywhere with air-conditioning' was looking rather last century. The resentment that had smouldered in the local architectural community since the 1970s now festered as a tangible grievance: criticism of the work of overseas-based architects had always been taken with a pinch of salt – Singaporean architects could not compete for the large jobs, so they were jealous – but it could now be asserted that the foreigners did not understand what they were doing in the tropics, and that they were flying in the face of a sustainable future. As can be imagined, this rhetoric meant little to many of those who financed large commercial developments, and swathes of cold-climate office towers – cocooned in reflective glass – are still being built in a city one degree north of the equator, but the wind is now categorically blowing in the other direction.

Contemporary society suffers from a devastating sickness. Mechanisation, which should have been a remedy for all its ills, has been misplaced. We allowed it to upset our traditional mode of life with which it was unable to come to terms.

Le Corbusier (1941)[4]

Tropical architecture in Singapore, as in all other Southeast Asian cities, is faced at all turns by a single basic dilemma: the fundamental principles – avoiding intense sunlight, sheltering from heavy rain, and providing constant ventilation – are anti-urban. The ideal tropical residence or place of work was a breezy shaded lightweight hut sitting beneath a canopy of trees (a 'type' adapted successfully by the British East India Company in the 17th century as the bungalow), but such structures were hardly practicable for densely populated townships. Sir Stamford Raffles designated the shophouse as the preferred residential/commercial type for the newly settled Singapore, which was a qualified success – the shophouses were dark and gloomy, but they were cool and required relatively little maintenance – but nobody will ever say that the shophouse is

4 Le Corbusier, *Sur les Quatres Routes*, Gallimard, NRF, Paris, 1941. As quoted by Kenneth Frampton in his essay 'The other Le Corbusier: primitive form and the linear city 1929-52', published in *Le Corbusier: Architect of the Century*, Arts Council of Great Britain, London, 1987. p29. In his text (p31), Frampton refers to early 1930s projects "... [that] seem to have served as metaphors for a non-doctrinaire future in which men could be free to combine primitive and sophisticated techniques according to their needs and resources," and to early 1940s housing that proposed grass-covered roofs and rammed-earth walls.

the tropical ideal, although the prototype spread throughout the nascent cities of the region. What a relief it must have been when air-conditioning became universally available, just as the colonial settlements grew up into cities whose living and working environments would require constant cooling. Singapore could now have the same architecture as Minneapolis and Melbourne, which it duly received, but – as with fossil-fuelled automobiles – nobody was to know that they were living in a fool's paradise. Massive cities sprung up in some of the world's hottest locations, with architects and planners (and immigrants) assuming that air-conditioning would at least keep the residents cool, if not dry. But as every planner and developer now knows that alternatives need to be considered, and as every architect working in a tropical city now understands the obligation to reduce the dependency, one must ask the question: why are so many buildings in tropical cities still being designed that do not even pay lip-service (in terms of their massing and external cladding) to notions of passive heat control and energy saving? Wrapping an apartment block or an office tower with LEED approved glass may satisfy quantifiable pre-requisites, but the approach (and the message it sends out) is fundamentally flawed. There are other ways to design tropical buildings, and there always have been, despite the existence of air-conditioning: the AXA Life Building (1975, by James Ferrie & Partners), for example, was shielded and cooled by a sculptural screen of twisted concrete blades, and looks far more comfortable in its skin than most of the recent highly-publicised landmark projects.

AXA Life Building

The most rewarding approach to tropical architecture in the 21st century may well be elemental rather than technological, producing buildings that are monumental and green, and which denote an almost primal reversion to natural ventilation and ubiquitous shading. The Clarke Quay redevelopment (2006) by Will Alsop was almost a caricature – a Pixar version – of what can be done to shade and ventilate large spaces in a tropical city: massive diaphanous umbrellas soar above two intersecting streets of restored shophouses, which are cooled by anthropomorphic over-scaled fans. The 'back to basics' ventilation of an outdoor precinct of bars and restaurants was one thing, however, but the creation of naturally and acceptably cooled large-scale buildings in a tropical city was quite another, and this is perhaps the holy grail of 21st century architecture. One imagines that, in due course, an indisputably sustainable compromise between artificial cooling and natural cooling will be reached, and many recent buildings in Singapore – notably Ken Yeang's National Library and his Solaris office building (2010) – have implemented programs of that nature. Two institutional buildings, however, stand out as genuine prototypes in the quest for the grail: the Khoo Teck Puat Hospital (2010 by RMJM Hillier with CPG Consultants) and the School of the Arts (2010 by WOHA). The buildings are resplendently cloaked with foliage, the massing and the spaces were manipulated to channel any available breezes through the public areas, and new ground planes were layered throughout the volumes. The classroom blocks on the top six levels of the eleven-storey arts school are all one-room-thick, so air-conditioning is unnecessary, whilst the hospital encouraged natural ventilation wherever possible. Both buildings have been specifically calibrated as structures that draw the best out of nature, whilst protecting the occupants from the worst.

School of the Arts (2010), WOHA

Khoo Teck Puat Hospital (2010), RMJM Hillier with CPG Consultants

Clarke Quay (2006), Alsop Architects with RSP Architects

Booth

Terminal Four... A Contradiction or Three

On March 24, 2012, an article entitled 'Flap over Changi Airport Terminal 4 Design Contest' appeared in The Straits Times... *"The job was to design the new Terminal 4 at one of Singapore's most recognisable icons, Changi Airport. So local architects hit the roof when they were apparently told this: 'Only foreign firms need apply'. They claim that they were made to understand this during a meeting with the airport on March 14. Less than a week later, the Singapore Institute of Architects wrote a letter to the Changi Airport Group (CAG) chief executive, Mr Lee Seow Hiang, to protest. A copy was obtained by The Straits Times."* The letter, written to Mr Lee on March 20 by the President of the Singapore Institute of Architects, Mr Ashvinkumar, concluded with the request... *"The local architectural community will be most appreciative and thankful for your kind consideration in lifting the restriction for their participation in this design competition."* On March 29, 2012, (the Singapore-based) Channel News Asia reported... *"All architect firms with a good portfolio and track record are welcome to submit proposals for the upcoming Changi Airport Terminal 4 design tender – regardless of whether they are local or foreign firms. The clarification came after the boss of Changi Airport Group (CAG) met the Singapore Institute of Architects to clear the air over who can or cannot participate in the tender."*

Try reading between all those lines! Some did, and their thoughts were articulated on various blogsites. One contributor wrote... *"The tone of the letter from the Singapore Institute of Architects says it all. The fearful bootlicking, begging tone of the letter convinces me that they got what they deserve... the letter will end up in the dustbin where it belongs."* Another was equally derisive... *"Local architects? Jia sai la! They can't even design proper HDB flats and yet they want to design T4? Ha ha ha!"* And one voice of moderation observed *"... local architects, designers, and perhaps most significantly, local design and architecture students, are worried about whether this is a stand that a government made up of fellow Singaporeans is really OK with: discriminating against local designers just for the sake of it."*

The devil was in the detail, the Catch 22 provided in the Channel News Asia soundbite... *"All architect firms with a good portfolio and track record are welcome..."* And exactly how many Singapore practices could possibly have a track record of building large airport terminals that compares with their American or European counterparts? End of discussion. But the thinking (allegedly, if one follows the wording of the news reports and the correspondence between SIA and CAG) that lies behind the logic of the CAG's position is depressing: we appear to have a contradiction or three, cloaked by obfuscation, splashed with a dose of hypocrisy, and watered from a deep well

...We now have a critical mass [with] a good base of trained architects... so the megaprojects really should be fully designed by local architects... we have now reached that point.

Alfred Wong (1997).[5]

5 Excerpted from conversation at the SIA Roundtable on Contemporary Singapore Architecture (September 3, 1997). Published in *Contemporary Singapore Architecture*, Singapore Institute of Architects, 1998. p283. Alfred Wong (born 1930) set up Alfred Wong Partnership in 1957, and designed the National Theatre (1959, now demolished) and the Marco Polo Hotel (1968, also demolished). He served as SIA President from 1962 to 1966, and received the inaugural SIA Gold Medal in 1998.

of anger and resentment (if blogsites and hearsay are to be accorded sufficient credibility). The vicious circle of excluding local architects from landmark projects that began in the mid-1970s continues, but on purely architectural terms, one can no longer understand why. Most of Singapore's leading architects (and this evidence is hearsay) believe that the quality of local architecture is downplayed in their own country for reasons that have long passed their use-by date. Every large international firm with a proven track record had to begin somewhere, which would tempt one to think that their home nations or cities gave them an opportunity, or that another country recognised the quality of their idea (regardless of 'good portfolios'). And it might now be observed that several Singaporean practices have a global reputation for their large-scale architecture: one is almost loath to point this out, but WOHA won the World Transport Building of the Year Award at the World Architecture Festival in 2009, and followed this with the International Highrise Award in 2010, and the RIBA Lubetkin Prize in 2011. Surely the design of a terminal at Changi Airport is not beyond them, or any number of other design-oriented local practices, and it might be suggested that Changi Airport could benefit from a fresh set of eyes. However, it would appear that the issue may not be architectural, and any further discussion is probably best confined to the blogsites.

Keong Saik Road

Reclaiming Singapore

The Singaporean architect (whether a temporary or permanent practitioner) is obliged to deal with equatorial temperatures, extreme humidity, torrential rain, and a new circumstance: the city now plays a leading role on the global stage (from Third World to First in record time). So any architect, whether locally trained or flown in first-class from London or New York, should get both the climatic side of things and the new global order well and truly in place, or their designs are going to come up short. Singapore, far from being a bed of roses (due to its relatively buoyant economy) in the early 21st century, is proving to be a graveyard for the credibility of many foreign architects who have not ventured beyond formalistic essays conjured up in a temperate climate.

Possibly the greatest testimony to Singapore's collective resurgence – after the dark days of World War II and the departure of the colonial rulers – has been the systematic and prioritised provision of public amenity: health, housing, education and infrastructure. And, not coincidentally, the best architecture of the last decade has been institutional and infrastructural. As the world, and Asia in particular,

Bishan Public Library (2006), LOOK Architects

faces up to the 21st century realities of urban overcrowding, inadequate infrastructure and environmental degradation, Singaporean architects and planners have been cognisant of the presumed problems for a long time: you could say that it's in their DNA, as Singaporeans have been shoring up Singapore all their lives. The recently built arts schools – the LaSalle College of the Arts, the NTU School of Art, Design and Media, and the School of the Arts – are not just notable for their architectural virtuosity, but for their engagement with the city and/or the landscape, their passive environmental strategies, and possibly most significantly, the unambiguous prioritisation of education and individual achievement within the society. Similar observations could be made of the Bishan Library, several MRT stations and hospitals, public parks and remediation projects, and Pinnacle@Duxton, the colossal inner-city public housing project. The architectural prioritisation was always that of the user or the occupant, and by extension, the public welfare of the community at large.

The flipside has been a commercial architecture less concerned with social cohesion than with global city emplacement and personal vanity. Singapore has very few aesthetically interesting office towers, and very few that demonstrate any degree of environmentally responsible innovation. The same could be said of recent corporate developments in any large city, where the CBD is more or less viewed as an amorphous orthogonal blob, but Singapore is one degree north of the equator and reflective glass towers are not appropriate, either environmentally or functionally. Whether the fault lies with the architects (the design architects are nearly all overseas-based), the developers or the urban planners is hard to pin down, and it might be possible to blame all three. The incremental spread of the downtown office towers across the reclaimed land south of Marina Bay is defiantly non-Singaporean: the city has always thrived upon its small-scale interconnectivity, both commercially and socially, and these vast glass towers, surrounded by treeless plains baking in the heat, appear as visions from a dystopian fantasy. The historic Raffles grid has been superseded by 'billion dollar' sites with no street-life whatsoever – all social activities have been internalised or sucked underground to the public transport links – and which make no discernable contribution to the urban fabric, as their glass tower blocks are completely self-referential. What will become of all the reclaimed land that currently lies empty to the southeast of the city is unclear, but one hopes that a semblance of the spirit of Singapore might be reclaimed.

public and commercial

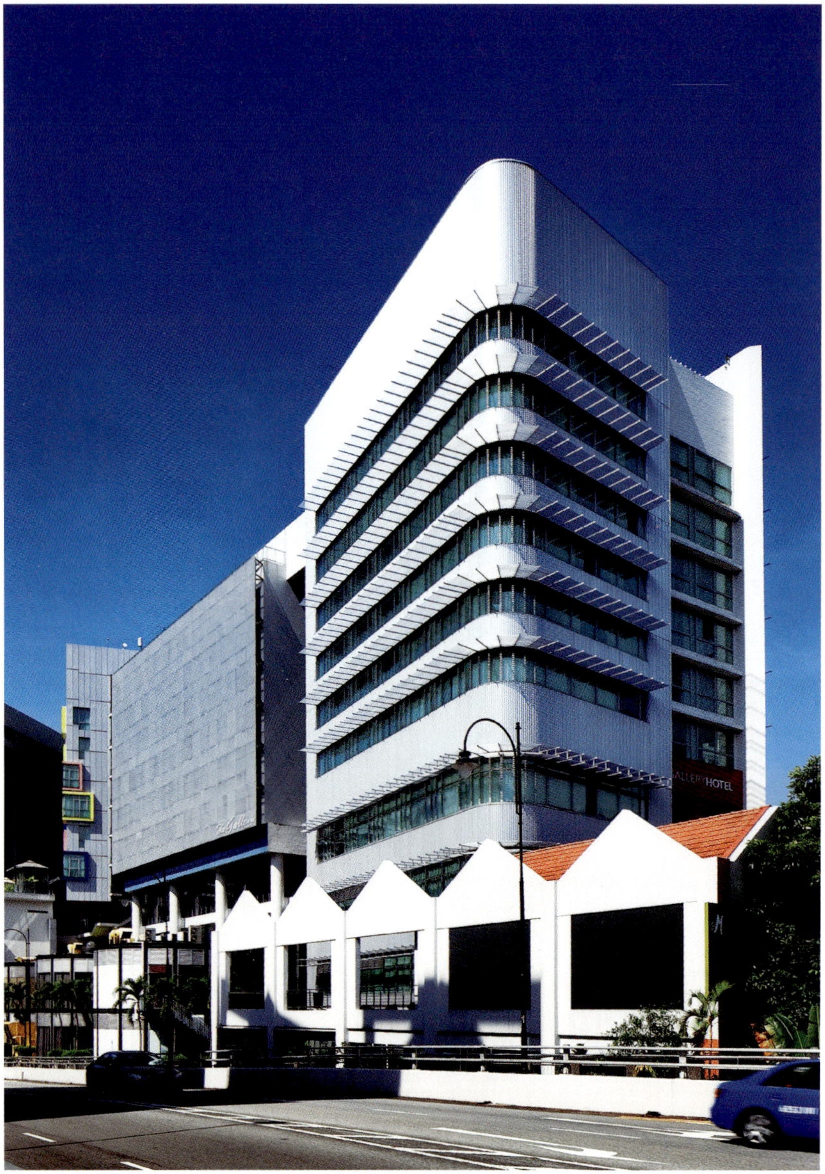

gallery hotel

nanson road
completed 2000
architect – william lim associates and tangguanbee architects

A whimsical collage of architectural references, this determinedly flamboyant hotel might appear to be a free-spirited work by a young and enthusiastic practice fired up by the potential impact of *outré* representational architecture as Singapore dusted itself off for the 21st century. But, indicative of the rather curious twists and turns performed by the city's architects over the previous twenty years, the building actually marked the end of an era. William Lim had been in practice since the 1950s, Tang Guan Bee from the 1960s, and both had been articulate and provocative champions of an architecture that has been variously described as quirky, eccentric and avant-garde, although Lim had also designed many houses that conscientiously engaged with their tropical context. Tang's best known buildings had displayed all the formal contradictions and non-local references that were to distinguish the Gallery Hotel. Lim had wholeheartedly embraced Post Modernism early in the piece with his bright pink Unit 8 condominium (1983), and continued to chart a local course through the subsequent tangents of colourful representational architecture.

The coming together of the two architects produced a work that is perhaps more resolved than any of their individual public projects: the collaborators, one surmises, kept each other's more wayward impulses in check. The hotel comprises a collection of deliberately discordant buildings, with a variety of façades, plans, materials and decorative details. A set of five blank gabled walls facing the street refers back – in a decidedly Post Modern ironic gesture – to the warehouses that previously occupied the riverfront site, and the street frontage is then continued with three two-storey metal cylinders, occupied by restaurants and clubs. A gleaming minimalist aluminium tower defines the hotel when seen across the river, a cantilevered box of hotel rooms with protruding (and extremely colourful) window-frames is placed diagonally on the northern edge of the complex, and these two structures are linked by a third block of rooms, demurely hidden behind a veil of steel mesh. Neither architect was to design another building of such significance, and the following generation(s) of local architects have more or less rejected the architecture of artifice, passing the torch of eccentricity and flamboyance to visiting architects.

The *parti* for this above ground railway station is almost amusingly simple: an elongated stainless steel carapace (or tortoise shell, if you like) covers the platform, supported by V-shaped columns and overlapped by an inverted disc at the entrance. The polished metal soffit of the carapace performs as a mirror within the station, so that reflected daylight is dispersed throughout the bright and capacious space. The disarming elegance and adroitness of the architecture is, quite undeniably, the work of an architectural practice at the peak of its powers: it may be only a cameo piece, as Foster and Partners had spent much of the past twenty designing significant portions of the world's transport infrastructure at a grand scale, but what a cameo piece. One can almost imagine the architects relaxing after another tortuous mega-structure session and turning to the Expo Station project with a sense of relief and glee: here we can do what we love to do. Not exactly back to basics, but a freedom from constraint and an opportunity for clear architectural expression, like a quick sketch from a master painter. The balance between the carapace and the disc is spoiled somewhat by the rudimentary concrete supports for the elevated railway line – there is always that sense of initial disappointment when a wonderful piece of architecture has been compromised by its context – but compensation lies in the structure's *sui generis*.

expo mrt station

changi south avenue 1
completed 2001
architect – foster and partners

changi airport mrt station
terminals 2 and 3, changi airport
completed 2002
architect – skidmore, owings and merrill

An elegant, understated (and curiously under-publicised) pedestrian link between Terminals 2 and 3 runs through a tunnel beneath the spine of Airport Boulevard as a 140-metre bridge, which forms a broad and lengthy shallow arch over the railway platforms below. This underground crossing is surprisingly suffused with daylight, which floods down through massive glass atria attached to the terminals at either end. As Skidmore, Owings and Merrill also designed Terminal 3, the architectural language of impeccably detailed glass and grey steel merges seamlessly at that connection, as it also does with the recently upgraded Terminal 2 (2006, by RSP Architects). The glass deck and arch of the bridge are lit from within, so that the steel-walled tunnel has a softly glowing ambience twenty-four hours a day. The terminal to terminal promenade is a sleek, symmetrical and impersonal netherworld, unsullied by colour and commercial intrusion, and suggests a Vorticist vision of dynamic efficiency (only usually seen in the idealised universe of businessman-on-the-move advertising).

esplanade – theatres on the bay

esplanade drive
completed 2002
architect – dp architects with
michael wilford and partners

In socio-architectural terms, this building was a milestone for Singapore: the country had pulled itself back from the edge of an economic and political abyss in 1965, and by 1990 had transformed itself into a First World country with a living standard the envy of Southeast Asia. The time was now ripe for the construction of a performing arts centre, which would serve as the materialist embodiment and an international symbol (or icon, to use current jargon) of the country's emergence and presumed maturity. A fabulous cultural edifice has come to represent, for better or for worse, newly acquired civic pride in cities from Paris to Dallas and from Sydney to Manaus, and the construction process of those landmarks was often as interesting (politically and socially) as the resultant architecture.

The Esplanade complex was originally designed in 1993 by the English architect Michael Wilford (long time partner of the late James Stirling) in conjunction with a local practice, DP Architects, but the initial representations showed massive glass enclosures without any apparent form of sun shading. Public complaint asserted that the building looked too Western and needed extensive protection from the tropical glare (which possibly amounted to a single criticism), and Michael Wilford left the project in the hands of DP Architects in 1995. DP worked closely with the engineering company, Atelier One, to create the now highly distinctive cladding system of triangular aluminium sun shields, which wrap around the two glass shells of the theatres. Closed sun shields were placed on the roof of the domes, and they gradually open up as they descend to reveal more of the view from the theatre foyers, and to admit late afternoon light. The spiky surface of the two shells has elicited many anthropomorphic comparisons, and the panorama of the pattern is best viewed internally, from the foyers of the Concert Hall and the Lyric Theatre (external views are compromised, unless you have a suite in a neighbouring high-rise hotel, as the complex is ringed by dense groves of palm trees and hidden by rain trees from a distance). The two shells splay apart from each other at 135 degrees, and a link between the theatres connects the low-roofed entry lobby to a shopping mall, which appears as a less than noteworthy extension on the bayside. It is a shame that something so architecturally prosaic has become the public (Marina Bay) face of the building, whilst the intricate western elevation lingers in relative obscurity: if only the plan could now be rotated 180 degrees. As to whether the structure lived up to 'global landmark' expectations is now a moot point, as so many other Singaporean edifices have popped up over the last decade, but the complex has been a notable success as a venue: it has proved unremittingly popular and is unreservedly cherished by the community at large.

st mary of the angels

bukit batok east avenue 2
completed 2003
architect – woha

Although increasing well known within the local architectural community for a string of imaginative and crisply detailed houses built in the 1990s, WOHA was a small practice and, one would have thought, unlikely candidates for what turned out to be a large-scale assignment for the Franciscan order: the master planning and design of a new church, monastery, columbarium and car park, and the renovation of the friary and parish centre. The spacious site sat comfortably on top of a small hill in Bukit Batok, surrounded by HDB housing towers, and thus presented an ideal location for what might be termed a 'complex' (typologically similar to a resort or campus). The architects assumed control of every aspect of the design – architecture, landscaping, interior design, furniture and lighting – so the overall ambience of restrained elegance is never compromised. The church itself is distinguished by a startlingly thin roof, which projects over the central courtyard to provide shelter, and by the sophistication of its joinery. The columbarium is lit from above through square skylights, which were cut out from the ramped garden rising west from the church, and a small onyx-clad bell-tower containing a chapel sits at the southern edge of the courtyard, which is flanked by screened colonnades. The completed architecture was greeted with much admiration by the architects' regional peer group, seen as an effortless and masterful appropriation of a European (especially northern European) style to its local context: the architecture looks like Scandinavian modern, but it is totally attuned to the tropics.

national library

victoria street
completed 2005
architect – t.r. hamzah & yeang
with dp architects

Descriptions and commentary of Ken Yeang's architecture tend to read as variations upon the same piece, so much the same that the articulation of his principles of ecological climate-responsive design has possibly become over-familiar, which may well obscure the objective appreciation of his buildings as architectural objects. Yeang has been an environmental evangelist since the 1970s, and his proselytising has categorically borne fruit. He has been admonishing his fellow professionals for so long and so successfully that further tub-thumping is no longer necessary, at least in terms of receiving the message (whether architects, developers and governmental authorities choose to heed the message is beyond his control). He has, however, designed and built relatively few projects, although several have been highly publicised and assimilated, such as the Menara Mesiniaga (Subang Jaya, Malaysia, 1992) and the UMNO Tower (Penang, Malaysia, 1998).

Won in competition, the National Library comprises two blocks (one for exhibitions and cultural activities, and another for the library and reading rooms) separated by a large atrium, which also acts as a pedestrian connection through the square full-block corner site in Bras Basah. As the two blocks and the atrium are mutually roofed, and conjoined by thin horizontal blades at every second level, the library reads as one building, and although only sixteen storeys high, it commands a highly visible presence in the skyline, looming over its predominantly low-rise neighbours. In a rather prosaic response to the proportions of the site, the structure has a cube-like massing, which was then deconstructed by an animated layering of sunshading devices, and recessed gardens and terraces. Yeang's commitment to sustainable ecological architecture and low energy principles determined every aspect of the design and the operation of the building, where various combinations of air conditioning and natural ventilation, and of natural and artificial lighting, can be utilised as required. The southwestern facade is a blank windowless wall, shielding the occupants from the afternoon sun (a technique used by Yeang to block the morning sun in his earlier UMNO Tower), which although admirable as a means of solar protection, is possibly questionable as an urban gesture. The white steel cladding was a curiously conservative choice, as it bestowed a disconcertingly corporate appearance to a prominent public building, but an amusingly retro-styled rooftop pod on the eastern corner supplies a perky and pert focal point for the surrounding area.

supreme court

supreme court lane
completed 2005
architect – foster and partners
with cpg consultants

The original Supreme Court, a stately domed neo-classical edifice with a grand aspect overlooking the Padang, was completed to the designs of Frank Dorrington Ward in 1939, just in time for World War II and the British surrender. As a symbol of Imperial hubris it could hardly be improved upon, and this wonderful folly is to be incorporated within the new National Art Gallery (by Studio Milou with CPG Consultants). The existing building had been adjudged as too small by the 1980s, and although additional courtrooms were constructed in the adjoining City Hall, the decision was taken to build a new Supreme Court on a site across a small laneway to the west. Norman Foster's design is most memorable for its 'flying saucer' disc-like form on the roof, which aspires to a yin-yang relationship with the dome of the 1939 building, and, as a rather esoteric local gesture, appears as a variation upon Foster's Expo MRT Station (2001) fifteen kilometres to the east. As the site was compact, the building has no setbacks and is wrapped on three sides by a modern version of the five-foot-way. The fourth side abuts a nondescript shopping mall, and the main frontage of the courthouse looks across North Bridge Road to more shopping centres, which although lively and popular, do not possess much in the way of civic gravitas. The beautifully detailed walls of the Supreme Court, clad in transparent Portuguese *rosa aurora* marble, appear to be slumming it for the time being. The internal blocks receive daylight from a central atrium and from skylights above the broad circulation routes, which rise through a series of escalators to the appellate court in the crowning disc. As the complex is so hemmed in by the mass of neighbouring buildings and screened so comprehensively by a canopy of rain trees, its civic presence is surprisingly insubstantial at street level, but its place in the cityscape is enshrined by the great inverted cupola.

one george street

completed 2005
architect – skidmore, owings and merrill

Due to its location on the southern edge of the low-rise Boat Quay/Circular Road precinct and the eastern edge of Hong Lim Park, One George Street is one of Singapore's most prominent office towers, although only twenty-five storeys in height. It is also conspicuous for its New York style massing, which stands in contrast to the sheer verticality of its neighbours in the city's northern CBD. The apparent setbacks in the tower's profile are not part of a strategy to prevent overshadowing at street level (never seen as a problem in a tropical city): they were cut out from the building's envelope to create sky gardens on the upper floors, and a large terrace (with swimming pool, gym and jogging track) on the fifth floor. The curtain wall is clad with a finely-detailed second skin of extruded aluminium rods, which discreetly veils the robust massing, and which shimmers in the heat of a bright sunny day. The building is crowned by a five-floor empty volume, and as the tower appears rather truncated for the size of its base and for the broadness of its proportions, it does not appear inconceivable that further vertical extension will take place.

E1

republic polytechnic

woodlands avenue 9
completed 2006
architect – maki and associates
with dp architects

The Republic Polytechnic, located just across the water from Johor in Singapore's northernmost suburb, is a tertiary institution offering a variety of courses aimed specifically at industrial vocations. The architecture is suitably rational and prosaic, with Fumihiko Maki's *parti* ordering every element and relationship on the campus. A continuing theme in the work of Maki, a Japanese architect who won the Pritzker Prize in 1993, is the creation of a civic order, which (to paraphrase Kenneth Frampton) avoids both gratuitous aestheticism and simple-minded functionalism. The *parti* saw the emplacement of a large single level ground-floor space (known as the Agora) beneath a grass roof, through which twelve cubic learning blocks rise on a grid within an elliptical plan. The site slopes gently down a hillside, so the rigour of the grid is slyly animated by the subtle changes to the sectional arrangements of the buildings and sunken gardens as the roof descends. The planning is ingenious and the landscaping beautiful, if rather manicured for a student environment, but the overall impression is not that of a tropically responsive piece of architecture. This is not to denigrate the intention, nor to advocate the prescription of a specific approach to architecture in Singapore, but one does suspect that the project could have been built anywhere in the world. Some of the teaching blocks are sheathed in sun-shading devices, but others have been left without, and they have, somewhat predictably, weathered rather badly. In formal terms, the Republic Polytechnic is an intentionally prototypical three-dimensional master plan, and one looks forward to seeing the ideas adapted and recalibrated (without such reliance upon air conditioning) to the local environment.

singapore management university

stamford road
completed 2006
architect – edward cullinan and knta

Comprising six blocks of buildings – scattered across Bras Basah Park and (for the most part) camouflaged by rain trees – the university campus has an amorphous presence in one of Singapore's most significant inner city precincts. Whether such evanescence can ever be a satisfactory urban gesture should possibly be the subject of an existential debate rather than a planning one, but the intention and resolution of the SMU scheme is undeniably curious. The six blocks are connected below street level, which whilst providing ease of access and autonomous communication within the campus, has resulted in an almost eerie absence of street life: a circumstance quite at odds with its position in the city and with the shaded amenity of the rain trees. The architectural forms appear almost hesitant, as if the architects were unsure as to whether they should defer to the parklands or assert a monumental presence. The elevations demonstrate an accretion of forms – curvaceous, streamlined, stratified and angular – capped by tiled skillion roofs that add a domestic element to the mixture. A top-heavy massing is created by the tapering of the building envelope from the solid projecting blocks of the upper floors down to the almost dainty columns at the base. Many of the elevations are wallpapered with greenery, a gesture that now looks rather more decisive and responsive than the architectural bricolage of the complex as a whole.

national musuem of singapore

stamford road
completed 2006
architect – cpg consultants
and w architects

The National Museum was originally built in 1887 to the neo-classical design of H.E. McCallum and J.F.A. McNair of the Public Works Department. Three subsequent alterations and additions were carried out before the decision was made in 2000 to double the capacity whilst simultaneously restoring the existing structure. The museum remains quite small, and the alterations and additions can be seen clearly: a second floor corridor on the central axis of the existing museum leads to a three-level modern addition. This new wing runs parallel to the long neo-classical pavilion that forms its eastern wall, and the large open spaces are lit from above through an extensive glass roof. As the roof of the connecting corridor was also glazed, providing views to 19th century dome, the museum feels wonderfully bright and capacious. So as to avoid disturbing the existing roofline, further exhibition space in the extension was created with a lower basement floor and in a three-storey glass drum at the southern end. The new wing can be entered on its third level from Fort Canning Park, through a rectangular façade screened with mesh (resembling a rather chic shipping container), and the circulation path through the museum was envisaged as a link between Bras Basah Park and Fort Canning, although it would appear that the Fort Canning entrance is rarely used: the original neo-classical portico is clearly too welcoming to resist.

the school of art, design and media – nanyang technological university

nanyang avenue 3
completed 2006
architect – cpg consultants

As one of the few buildings in Singapore that had the chance to respond to topographical conditions – and actually did so – the *parti* of the arts school is understood at first sight: three intertwined embankments, covered with grass and forming the roofs of the curving blocks below, rise up as great scything arcs within a broader landscape of low forested hills. The Nanyang Technological University campus, in the northwest of the island, has grown incrementally since 1955 (when the land was donated by the Hokkien Huay Kuan clan) and the relatively laidback ambience is that of an environment far removed from the city. The arts school reflects that (very non-Singaporean) dislocation with a structure that is non-urban, whose features are not provocative, and whose forms are not determined by the need to solve a problem. The glazed blocks of classrooms surround an elliptical landscaped courtyard, and the circuitous circulation routes befit a school with a wide range of creative programs, where contemplation, spontaneity and dynamic interaction are to be valued. The building should simply be seen as piece of monumental inhabitable land art, whose scale, vanishing points and swirling geometries are quite surreal. Architecture as art can still play a role, especially when it is carpeted with a sustainable roof.

vivocity

telok blangah road
completed 2006
architect – toyo ito with
dp architects

Despite its waterfront location, the site for Singapore's largest shopping mall was an awkward one: cramped on its northern entry elevation by a brutal overhead expressway, and difficult to visualise for the passerby. Although Toyo Ito's complex has been praised for its internal spatial flow, the exterior undoubtedly required a stronger formal response – an eye-catching structure that would have established a recognisable shape for the building – as the low-slung three-storey mass slumps as an inert presence, seemingly built to conform to zoning requirements without further consideration. The mall's publicity claims that the design 'evokes images of waves in the sea' (a waterfront design cliché), but the wave-like gestures are timid, confined to stairways and balustrades. The roof is entirely given over to public space, but the design elements (tubular latticework and so on) only serve to camouflage the service blocks, and, without extensive shading, the roof is just too hot to be useful. The car park – with walls of white undulating concrete punctured by elliptical voids – is the public face of VivoCity, but for some reason the surface is very badly rendered and covered with patches. The fluid circulation through the shopping plaza is, however, the project's saving grace, and as VivoCity is so unequivocally popular, the development must be deemed a success, but one suspects that sculptural and structural remediation cannot be too far down the track.

mint toy museum

seah street
completed 2006
architect – scda

The façade– a sculpted sliver of undulating glass fins – of this small gallery has a playful presence within a gritty, rather rundown streetscape that, somewhat incongruously, flanks the northeastern elevation of the Raffles Hotel. The Mint Toy Museum (an acronym for Moment of Imagination and Nostalgia with Toys) was inserted within the five levels of a particularly slender shell, as a building within a building above an entry lobby and wine-bar at street level. The rippling façade requires little in the way of explanation, as the arrangement and formation are self-evident, but the urban gesture – the almost casual interpolation of a piece of public art within an uncodified city precinct – is worth a moment's thought. As a recently anointed First World city, Singapore has dutifully discarded the garish building frontages and the proudly ephemeral urbanity of the tropical Asian city in favour of a decorous heterogeneity, but as part of the process, displays of 'architecture as art' have also gone missing. The Mint Toy Museum signals a potential new direction for urban Singapore, one which so illuminates the low-rise streetscapes of Europe, where boutiques and galleries with jewel-like façades and crafted protrusions rub shoulders with the city's foot soldiers.

clarke quay
clarke street
completed 2006
architect – alsop architects
with rsp architects

Singapore only exists because of its value as a port, the pivot between the Malacca Straits and the South China Sea, and the Indian and Pacific Oceans beyond. The maritime activities had always been carried out in the surprisingly small Singapore River, which was so crowded and polluted by the 1970s that it had become dysfunctional as a port and a health risk to the rapidly modernising city. In 1977, Lee Kuan Yew announced a scheme to clean up the river: shipping was relocated to Pasir Panjang west of the city centre (thus instigating an ultimately massive expansion along the length of the west coast), all associated industry and housing was relocated, the river was thoroughly dredged and remediated, and within ten years the Singapore River was once again a clean tidal waterway. Clarke Quay, along with Robertson Quay further upstream, had been the warehouse district, receiving goods from Boat Quay by barge lighters, and the newly freed-up precinct was always ripe for an autonomous regeneration as it occupied a pocket of land (200 metres wide by 300 metres) enclosed by a loop of the river. The Clarke Quay Festival Village (opened in 1993) was the first significant attempt to breathe new life into the riverfront, but the potential of the site was such that a major upgrading was inevitable, and Will Alsop was chosen to shake things up in 2002.

Alsop, an English architect whose colourful, unusual, amusing and highly practical forms reflect his oft-quoted comment... "I like people. I hope it shows..." was possibly the perfect choice for the redevelopment. And so it has proved. Any carping has been of the gratuitous variety by recidivist critics. The architectural forms and individual features – such as the lily-pad restaurant pods lining the riverfront and the lotus root 'faces' of the cooling fans – are witty, whimsical and inspired, but the substantial achievements were the shading of the open areas and the respect paid to the historic streetscapes. Clarke Street and Read Street, which run the width and length of the site and intersect at the centre, were covered with huge transparent 'umbrellas' to keep out the rain and screen the sun, with large low-speed fans mounted on the framework to blow breezes through the streets. The shophouses and warehouses were brightly painted, but in a such a theatrical setting their appearance is in the spirit of a carnival: the colour does not seem garish, and harks back to the ornate decoration of local Straits architecture. The only cloud on the horizon is, of course, one of durability. For how long – both architecturally and socially – can Clarke Quay remain vibrant?

bishan public library

bishan place
completed 2006
architect – look architects

One of Singapore's most acclaimed recent buildings, the Bishan Library derives much of its qualities from a combination of conventional architectural form with highly unconventional and unexpected features: a straightforward methodology that has characterised the work of Look Boon Gee since he established LOOK Architects in 1993. By calibrating the degree of innovation within a formal framework, the architecture is readily understood by the public, who can then revel in the decorative surprises and compositional delights. The Bishan Library is essentially a solid cube with a glazed northern elevation, shielded by a parasol roof and raised on a small podium, which provides the building with an aspect of (suburban) civic decorum in the face of the adjoining shopping mall and public car park. The unforgettable image of the library is provided by ten glazed vertical pods – coloured green, blue or yellow – that pop out from the northern façade as private, though very public, reading rooms. As a result of this exercise in structural and compositional whimsy, the library is now known island-wide and has become something of an icon for the heartlands (the local description for the housing estates where most Singaporeans live). More pods of coloured glass overlook an internal atrium, which contains gently sloping ramps between floors and provides filtered natural daylight. This sun-filled void forms part of a network of free-flowing shared spaces, and can be seen as an extension of the community spirit that characterises suburban Singapore, where studying in the library is as integral to daily life as going to the market or eating chicken rice. Look Boon Gee is fundamentally attuned to local life and local expectations, and appears intent upon providing an architecture – both clever and delightful – that genuinely contributes to, and may actually constitute, the new urban landscape of Singapore.

Library

AL-MUKMININ MOSQUE
MUKMININ MOSQUE

al mukminin mosque

jurong east street 21
completed 2006
architect – forum architects

A prayer hall with a decahedral roof form, pinched up as though it were a napkin, was originally built in 1987 on the flatlands of the Jurong new town. An extension, comprising a four-storey *madrassah* (an Islamic study centre) wraps around the prayer hall with a curved screen: an arabesque of blue, turquoise and yellow aluminium louvres. The traditional colouration forms part of a contemporary interpretation of Islamic architectural principles, where a dematerialisation between masses and elements symbolises the ephemeral nature of barriers. And, of course, the permeable wall encourages ventilation and protects the *madrassah* from the afternoon sun. The eastern elevation –facing directly onto a main road and an elevated railway – features a blank façade with a geometric pattern, beautifully delineated in stainless steel and framed by a rectangular concrete shell. A slender minaret, also composed of steel and concrete, flanks the eastern façade as part of a composition that recalls both the heydays of International Modernism and the intricacies of Islamic decoration.

entrance plaza to singapore
science centre

science centre road
completed 2006
architect – forum architects

The Singapore Science Centre was designed by Raymond Woo and opened in 1977, and then extended, with the inclusion of an omniplanetarium, by the same architect in 1987. The complex had begun to show its age, and although of interest to historians of a semi-heroic period in local architecture (which also produced the neighbouring Jurong Town Hall by Architects Team 3 in 1974), it required visual rebranding to attract attention (at least in the short term, as plans to relocate the complex are in place). Although the existing buildings were geometrically complex, they were clad in a common grey, so the approach by Forum Architects to attract attention was unambiguous, to say the least: the arrival forecourt would now be as colourful as possible, and presented as an 'installation' rather than architecture. The new entrance plaza disassociated itself completely from the architecture, both as a gesture of respect and as a means of establishing a completely fresh ambience (apart from two tapering silver columns that marked the formal entry to the centre). Trapezoidal panels of coloured laminated glass were placed in a sequence of three modules (derived from the Fibonacci Series) upon five steel shelves to form elongated kaleidoscopic walls. The colours range across the spectrum, and the composition has a dynamic diagonal Futurist energy, which might hopefully be redeployed elsewhere (perhaps a public park?) at some point in the future, as the current car park context is rather dispiriting.

hortpark visitor centre
hyderabad road
completed 2007
architect – mkpl architects

HortPark (a 'knowledge hub for plants and gardening') forms part of the nine-kilometre Southern Ridges trail, which wends from Mount Faber in the east to Kent Ridge Park in the west, and features the Henderson Waves Bridge and the Forest Walk. The Visitor Centre follows on from the Forest Walk, by LOOK Architects, and extends that walkway's aesthetic of lightweight but robust engineering with a pavilion comprising black-painted steel columns and a floating roof, which admits daylight through a central sky-lit screen of timber battens. Raised on a plinth above the gardens, this completely open and breezy structure is unabashedly modernist, rectangular in plan with a sharp-edged delineation of elements: a notably non-Singaporean approach to tropical architecture, and one more readily identified with the Mediterranean climates of Australia and Southern California. Such a lightweight pavilion is not really suitable for any purpose other than a transit point or an information centre in Singapore, as the local environment – and all that it may contain – could wreak havoc upon the inhabitants, but it is refreshing to see such clean open lines against the forest backdrop. A similar typological exercise by Kerry Hill Architects – The Entrance Plaza at Singapore Zoo (2003) – has been completely obliterated by a series of accretions and alterations over the past decade (another cautionary tale of the fate that can befall minimally-detailed elegant structures in Singapore).

changi airport terminal 3

airport boulevard
completed 2007
architect – skidmore, owings
and merrill with cpg consultants

Changi Airport opened in 1981 as part of Singapore's unflinching determination to capitalise upon one of its few natural advantages: its almost unrivalled location for travel and transportation. Perched at the southern tip of the Malay Peninsula, at the pivotal point between the Malacca Straits and the South China Sea, it had always (unavoidably) been a significant port, but the island was very well placed for air-travel, both within the region and as a hub for long-haul flights between Europe, Australia, northern Asia and North America. The hub would become, inevitably, the excuse for a Singapore stopover and shopping excursion, and the economy would flourish. And so it came to pass. The first two terminals (Terminal 1 was completed in 1981 and Terminal 2 in 1990) have been continually upgraded with the insertion of appropriately high-end interior spaces, but neither was originally conceived as fanciful architecture. Terminal 3, however, was conceptualised as a stand-alone piece of architecture, and whilst conforming to the existing airport's pervading ambience of understated elegance and aversion to formal attention-seeking (aside from the much-cherished control tower), its lofty departure hall is an exceptionally beautiful space. A steel-truss cable-braced roof with glass skylights supports a magnificent array of sensor-controlled aluminium louvres, which flutter across the width of the space with an ethereal diaphanous presence. A 300 metre-wide wall of greenery (by Tierra Design) rises from the baggage collection level to the roof, between the check-in areas and the immigration zone. The air-side precinct is one great shopping mall, which incorporates further planting and utilises warm timber detailing as a contrast to the silvered refinement of the omnipresent roof structure.

lasalle college of the arts
mcnally street
completed 2007
architect – rsp architects

Both a sculpted object and an extension of the city's urban fabric, the LaSalle College of Arts is a monumental building, which (possibly paradoxically) is completely accessible and welcoming to the community at large. Although fortress-like in appearance, the black exterior walls – inscribed with slot windows – simply serve to indicate where the six entrances to the large internal streets are located. As the college is sited between an HDB estate to the northwest, and markets and shops to the southeast, its internal streets are treated as thoroughfares by neighbouring residents, which contributes to what might be considered as the perfect ambience for an art college for young adults. The students are not cloistered away from the real world, as they can gaze down from the classrooms at curious backpackers and senior citizens returning from the markets. The interior of the building is quite a curiosity, as six contorted glazed blocks teeter above the communal streets, their contortions clearly articulated by black mullions. The white fabric roof looks rather insubstantial and unresolved in comparison to the rigorous geometry of the glazed blocks and the heavy presence of the external walls, but it does provide bright diffused light, lending a sharpness to the delineations of the internal structure. Bridges connect the blocks at various levels, and the circulation routes through the college appear to be deliberately difficult to comprehend: not a bad idea for an art college, where spontaneous, unexpected encounters are surely to be encouraged.

INNO
ATIVES

forest walk

telok blangah green
completed 2008
architect – look architects

Comprising the central section of the Southern Ridges Trail through the jungle from Mount Faber to Kent Ridge Park, the Forest Walk is a delightful excursion from nowhere to nowhere in particular, a journey to be had for the sake of the journey itself. The walk descends from the heights of Telok Blangah Hill (accessed from Mount Faber in the east by the Henderson Waves Bridge) through a shallow valley of rainforest to Alexandra Road, where it crosses the Alexandra Arch to link up with HortPark and to continue as the Canopy Walk to Kent Ridge. Never stepped, always ramped, the 1.6 kilometre Forest Walk is a beautifully conceived and detailed piece of engineering: made from galvanised steel, it has a delicate yet incisive presence as it zigzags down from Telok Blangah Hill and straightens out to proceed as a series of elevated promenades through the canopy of trees. A companion trail runs below on the floor of the valley. The perforated triangular panels of the walkway's deck took their cue from the local 'mile-a-minute' quick-growing creeper, distinguished by its equilaterally triangular leaves.

The Forest Walk should possibly be described as a phenomenological pathway, as its only concerns are with perception and experience. The twenty-minute walk is a completely visual, aural and tactile journey, and as any pedestrian movement (especially that of joggers) sets of a series of vibrations, it becomes an unexpectedly interactive trip. A process of reclaiming the landscape has emerged throughout Singapore in the last decade, with such like-minded projects as Punggol Promenade (also by LOOK), Bishan – Ang Mo Kio Park, and My Waterway@Punggol, with sensitive architectural components (basically bridges and lookouts) that can facilitate human curiosity whilst ensuring that nature is left well alone. Much attention has been paid to the disappearance of Singapore's architectural landscape over the last fifty years, which can never be remediated, but re-engagement with the natural landscape can be a salve of sorts (especially in the eyes of children, who are far more interested in trees, birds and animals than in buildings). Much of Singapore's industrial revolution of the 1960s and 1970s in Jurong was camouflaged by the creation of parks, such as the Singapore Bird Park (opened in 1971), a program continuing on the reclaimed lands south of the city centre, but discreet excursions into remaining pockets of wilderness and ameliorative proposals for abused waterways are the mark of a new sensibility: an acknowledgment that the city does not need architecture and landscaping as much as it needs nature.

genexis theatre

fusionopolis way
completed 2008
architect – woha

The three towers of the Fusionopolis complex cluster around a large egg-shaped metal-clad volume suspended three floors above ground level, which was intended to serve both as a venue for conventions, launches and seminars, and as a performance and exhibition space for the arts community, so that the one-north ambition of an elite environment of art integrated with science could be realised. The interior of the egg would thus need to be extremely flexible, adapting to a variety of seating and stage modes, but the insides of eggs are acoustically problematic, as the oval form directs sound to the centre of the space. WOHA, working with Arup Acoustic Consulting, came up with the ingenious notion of diffusing the sound with a massive set of wooden beads, which would line the internal circumference. 400,000 beads, hand-made in a village near Jakarta, were individually calculated for optimum acoustic performance: and with calibrated circular openings in the beads, the curved walls are now surfaced with a wonderfully tactile piece of timber joinery. The theatre in the egg is reached by escalator from a semi-circular lobby area in one of the towers, and the walls and ceilings of this foyer/pre-function space wrap over as waves of plywood fins, undulating in response to the curve of the floor plan. Brightly coloured trapezoidal seating – a wry comment on Zaha Hadid's master plan for the buildings of the surrounding one-north precinct – is scattered across a dark terrazzo floor.

fusionopolis

fusionopolis way
completed 2008
architect – kisho kurokawa
with jurong consultants

Comprising three towers with utopian appellations – Connexis North, Connexis South and Symbiosis – Fusionopolis forms part of the one-north vision of the future: a business park adjacent to Singapore National University, specialising in research and development, information technology and biomedical science. So what could more appropriate than commissioning one of the most visionary architects of the last fifty years: Kisho Kurokawa, a founder of the Metabolist movement, and designer of the 'plug-in' Nakagin Capsule Tower (1970-1972). The result, however, is rather underwhelming, and as a vision of the future, Fusionopolis leaves a lot to be desired.

The proportions are leaden, the profiles of each tower ars diminished by their proximity to one another (as demanded, apparently, by Zaha Hadid's one-north master plan), the composition of the elevations is clumsy, and the concave and convex plans appear to respond to nothing in particular. As with many other contemporaneous Singapore buildings by well-known international architects, the completed architecture is not bad 'product' as such, but the built form is very disappointing, and the initial design concept appears to be have been half-hearted (for whatever reason).

quincy hotel

mount elizabeth
completion 2008
architect – ong & ong

Perched on a narrow site at the top of a hill in an enclave of hotels and apartments near Orchard Road, the façade of Quincy Hotel is noteworthy for its pattern of subtly protruding windows. Each of the 108 rooms in the hotel is delineated by a four-metre-wide panel, which can be configured variously as a full-span window, or as a window with a bay-seat behind the wall (the window is two-thirds of the width and the wall one-third), or as further permutations thereof. With a projecting swimming pool on the twelfth floor added to the jigsaw, the façade pops up as an unexpectedly delightful presence in the narrow street. The vertical orthogonal volume itself is unremarkable, but the façade must perceived as a public artwork – a mosaic for the city – and as such, the decorative design does much to enliven the leaden appearance of an urban precinct that feels overbuilt and oppressive: thus performing a role that architecture often neglects to play.

singapore flyer

raffles avenue
completed 2008
engineer – arup
architect – kisho kurokawa
with dp architects

With a height of 165 metres, the Singapore Flyer was possibly the world's tallest ferris wheel (or giant observation wheel in current parlance) at the time of writing, and whilst under construction, invited endless comparisons with the London Eye (completed eight years earlier). London is a densely settled low-rise city with very few public vantage points – it does not have an Eiffel Tower or an Empire State Building – and the placement of the London Eye across the Thames from the centre of the city was ideal for viewing 350 years worth of architecture. As with the erection of the Eiffel Tower in 1889, debate as to the wheel's contextual fit appears to have been overwhelmed by its novelty and its provision of previously denied views. Conversely, the Singapore Flyer is a fine addition to the Singapore skyline, providing a focal point where the Singapore and Kallang Rivers nominally meet up in Marina Bay, but the aerial views are not unique or especially noteworthy. Singapore is a high-rise city, and as views could potentially be had from any number of towers, a wheel was not strictly necessary, and as the best views are of the city skyline, it could be argued that increased elevation is no great advantage. The location is curious, as one might have thought that the aerial views from a site further inland – revealing Singapore's historic urban fabric – would be more interesting than the panorama of unused reclaimed land lying to the east and south of the Flyer. A single revolution takes thirty minutes, and the wheel passes through a three-storey terminal building at the base. The symmetrical structure is a robust yet elegant piece of engineering, with twenty-eight barrel-shaped capsules externally attached to a ladder-truss rim, held in place by a web of spokes.

henderson waves

mount faber loop
completed 2008
architect – ijp architects
with rsp architects

Forming part of the Southern Ridges footway (linking Mount Faber, Telok Blangah Hill, Kent Ridge and West Coast Park), the Henderson Waves footbridge crosses thirty-six metres above Henderson Road in the valley between Mount Faber and Telok Blangah Hill. A kilometre to the west, the footway then descends into the Forest Walk (2008) by LOOK Architects: a no less beguiling, but certainly less flamboyant insertion into nature. An open international competition for a bridge over Henderson Road was won by the English architects IJP, with a scheme that overtly expressed a series of rippling waves, supported by slender concrete pylons. The three-dimensional waveform of metal ribs swells and recedes to create a series of seven perfect undulations, rising above and falling below the northern edge of the footway. The timber of the footway and of the curved banks of seating within the spiraling waves has weathered beautifully (in contrast, unfortunately, to the pale-yellow painted steel ribs, which are now coated with layers of grime). The form of the bridge, when seen on approach from Henderson Road or from the hillsides, constitutes a fantastic sculptural artefact, particularly as it can only be viewed against the sky and jungle-clad slopes. The views from the bridge are equally fascinating, a glimpse into the realities of Singapore, as the beautiful rainforest of the Southern Ridges is revealed to be a remnant: a surviving (though satisfyingly large) pocket of tropical vegetation, which gives way to the massive docklands of one of the world's busiest container ports.

bras basah mrt station

bras basah road
completed 2008
architect – woha

With little experience of large-scale design and none whatsoever of transport and infrastructure, WOHA won an open international competition held in 2000 for two MRT stations: Bras Basah and Stadium. In the interests of risk-minimisation, such open competitions were scrapped soon after these victories, but – largely as a result of these two commissions – WOHA were to quickly acquire an enviable track record for a local practice. As this enabled them to attract further large projects and establish a flourishing practice, one must question the wisdom of removing such an incentive for potentially visionary younger architects. And, it must be observed, that both the Bras Basah and Stadium stations are now perceived as two of Singapore's great urban experiences: an achievement realised only too infrequently by established architects with a quantifiable track record.

WOHA's design solution for the Bras Basah station was clear-sighted and ingenious. The site could not have been more precious to Singapore's civic heritage – framed by the Singapore Art Museum, the Cathedral of the Good Shepherd, and the National Museum – and the competition brief called for minimal visual intrusion upon this vista. WOHA's proposal was practically invisible at ground level, thus preserving the 19th century status quo, but it nonetheless constituted a monumental piece of architecture. A reflection pool, now part of the orderly landscaping of the precinct, sits upon a vast plane of glass, which serves as the roof of the station. Sunlight passes through this lake to the concourse level ten metres below, and bounces off a huge canted limestone wall to illuminate the platforms deep in the bowels of the earth (the MRT lines run at their lowest point at Bras Basah). The bounced light was required as the platforms were off-set to the east, below Bras Basah Road rather than the main volume of the station. Two sets of escalators scissor through the massive void between the concourse and the crossover level to the platforms, passing between cylindrical struts as part of what must be appreciated as a deliberately theatrical design, taking advantage of the plunging descent. As the water-dappled patterns of the sunlight constantly shimmer over the great limestone wall, the view looking up from the platforms and the crossover level is delightful and refreshing for a commuter. The underground spatial and structural innovations, complemented by a completely deferential (non) intervention at ground level, mark the resolution of an urban problem with an architecture that offers something unexpected and something uplifting.

crowne plaza hotel, changi airport

airport boulevard
completed 2008
architect – woha

By some distance the most conspicuous building at Changi Airport, where the seemingly decreed ambience is one of deference and discretion, the orthogonal Crowne Plaza Hotel is wrapped by screens of intertwined white polymer-gypsum ribbons as a representation of orchids in bloom. The tropical and floral motifs are continued throughout the interiors of the hotel, whose focal point is a lavish entrance lobby, wrapped by curvaceous timber-panelled walls and adorned with layers of batik fabrics, Thai tiles and coloured screens. The blocks of rooms sit on an S-shaped plan that encloses two third-floor garden courtyards, from which one can gaze up to the sky through a canopy of 'orchids' extended from the façades. The building is permeable and naturally ventilated: open air corridors run the length of the room blocks, and air-wells provide daylight to the rooms' bathrooms and entries. The structure is an elemental piece of sustainable architecture, camouflaged by an irresistibly flamboyant décor.

stadium mrt station

stadium walk
completed 2008
architect – woha

As with the Bras Basah MRT Station, the Stadium Station was won by WOHA in an open competition held by the Singapore Institute of Architects and the Land Transport Authority in 2000 for the design for two stations on the proposed Marina Line (now called the Circle Line). The original idea, the *parti*, for Stadium Station was so simple as to appear disingenuous: an early sketch shows two parallel brushstrokes, one straight and one curved, a railway track gone wrong. The lines were those of the two walls above the low-lying platform, with the convex wall deferring to the elliptical form of the adjacent National Stadium. This convex wall bulges out at the top, almost touching the straight wall to the south, and tapers to provide a broader space at the base. Daylight would have penetrated indirectly, as the station was to be placed underneath an elevated roadway, but in a serendipitous circumstance the road was diverted and the station could now be directly lit through a slender crescent-shaped skylight paced in the roof of an unobtrusive above-ground volume. The external and internal walls were clad in aluminium panels with finely incised rib-lines whose protrusions vary slightly, which was enough to create a sparkling shimmer throughout the interior. The station can be seen as a great silver canyon, at its best on a sunny day, when one can track the movement of the sun by the long strip of bright light that moves inexorably down the walls, across the platform level, and back up the other wall. The platform level floor is made up of quartz agglomerate panels of green, blue and aquamarine: a sea of blue and green at the base of a rather surreal, otherworldly environment.

ascott centre for excellence

anthony road
completed 2008
architect – look architects

The rehabilitation of the dilapidated former Chao Yang School at Newton Circus resulted in an idiosyncratic collection of pitched-roof pavilions that look more rural than urban, in a vernacular idiom not conspicuously redolent of Singapore. Four long pitched-roof buildings projected eastward from a connecting block, and the architects retained the forms whilst installing translucent skylights and over-sized vertical windows. The windows and skylights of each identical pavilion were encased within an articulated spine of orthogonal steel volumes, which rise above a flaring lightweight roof. As the short elevations are clad in timber, which has weathered and faded over the last few years, the compound of buildings – used as a regional training facility for an international serviced-residence operator – could be mistaken for a set of stables in the sweeping plains of Australia or America. It is assumed that the low-rise occupation of a large site in such a prized location will be temporary, so the vision of pastoral tranquility may well constitute little more than a footnote in the history of Singapore's architectural and urban discourse, but it does perhaps represent a whimsical musing as to what might have been. Singapore's almost exclusive embrace of orthogonal European modernism and the Southeast Asian vernacular style precluded the appropriation of many alternative forms of contemporary architecture, one of which was the urban interpretation of a rural archetype.

marina barrage

marina gardens drive
completed 2008
architect – team 3 architects

In order to 'harness the full potential of Singapore's waterways', the Public Utilities Board (PUB) launched its Active, Beautiful and Clean (ABC) Waters program in 2006, with the far-sighted ambition of treating all the island's water as one controllable self-sustaining resource. Barrages were built to create reservoirs at the mouths of rivers to control flooding in the city's low-lying areas, to form part of a fresh water treatment and supply system, and to provide safe bodies of water for recreational use. The Singapore and Kallang Rivers merge to form Marina Bay, which is separated from the sea by a barrage on the newly constituted shoreline: two and a half kilometres southeast of the original coast. The pumping station adjoining the barrage was viewed as an opportunity to provide both an educational facility to explain the ABC program and a recreational facility at the mouth of Marina Bay. The project was, thankfully, treated as a landscaping exercise rather than architecture, and a massive coiled grass-covered ramp forms a promenade, a roof and a park (which has become a serious kite-flying destination). The ramp takes the shape of the number 9 (the Chinese symbol of longevity) with a large elliptical concrete courtyard at its centre, which contains various interactive water features and a glimpse into the pump room. The barrage itself, however, represents a missed opportunity – it is little more than a rudimentary dam and a footbridge to the northeastern shore – when it could have formed an integral part of the project's monumental geometry.

wilkie edge

selegie street
completed 2009
architect – woha

The site for Wilkie Edge, which overlooks a major intersection, was surrounded by over-scaled residential blocks, rundown four-storey shophouses, a Sikh temple, undistinguished commercial buildings and low-rise remnants from an earlier era. Although the precinct possesses one of Singapore's most delightful and unexpected agglomerations of small-scale activities – retail and otherwise – the existing built landscape offered little to the architects in terms of architectonic reference, and an incremental abandonment of scale and proportion with each successive development effectively meant that no new project could tangibly engage with the urban context. Wilkie Edge formed a reflexive response to this environment, as the architects took it for granted that any assertive formal gesture would constitute a self-indulgent anti-urban escape from reality: what the *genius loci* required instead was a significant presence that might unify the disparate elements, or at least shore things up a bit. The forms of the building were fragmented, alternating between protrusion and void, as the mass of the building – veiled (in a sure sign of deference) by a silver aluminium screen – is carved open to reveal colourful terraces and rooftop gardens. A large 'media façade' (designed in collaboration with Berlin based realities:united) acts as a focal point for the precinct, which whilst not exactly Orchard Road, is thronged with shoppers and students at all hours.

iluma
victoria street
completed 2009
architect – woha

This shopping mall was intended to kick-start the revitalisation of the area between the Bugis neighbourhood and Selegie Road, which had been earmarked as an arts and entertainment district. The site sat opposite a relatively sedate collection of buildings on Victoria Street, but backed onto a scene straight out of the backpacker's guide to Southeast Asia: markets, rickshaws, durian vendors and food stalls, overlooked by garishly painted housing blocks. The architects responded to this dichotomy, and to that of the building's program, in a most straightforward way: they designed a building in two halves. The Victoria Street component has a 'seductive' curvaceous façade, festooned completely with spangled hexagons (a pattern developed with Berlin-based realities:united), which light up at night to perform as a flickering artwork. The Victoria Street façade steps back at various levels to accommodate outdoor terraces, whose plantings define the curvatures of the mass. The other half of iluma takes the form of a large orthogonal volume, clad with a screen of perforated red, orange and grey metal strips. The big box contains movie theatres and a carpark, whilst the sumptuous curves of the Victoria Street volume contain ten levels of shops and restaurants. The interior space of the shopping mall was spectacular – ten layers of undulating elliptical terraces overlooked an atrium with a swirling floor pattern inspired by Roberto Burle-Marx – but, astonishingly, it has been gutted after only two years of use. The eventual impact of iluma, with its less than subtle usage of colour, cladding and sculptural form has yet to be seen (Singapore has always had a demure approach to public and commercial architecture in comparison to its Asian neighbours), but the mall's strategy of engagement with the circulation routes of the city, providing through-routes as an extension of the precinct's laneways, is one from which all architects and planners must take heed.

capella resort

artillery avenue
completed 2009
architect – foster and partners with dp architects

As it protected Keppel Harbour, Sentosa Island was heavily fortified by the British, and two of the remaining 19th century military buildings (double-storey pavilions with pitched roofs of terracotta tiles) were conserved and incorporated within a high-end resort as the public areas of the hotel, at the crest of a hill overlooking the ocean. The colonnades of the colonial buildings link with the external arcades of a looping four-level modern extension, which is clad with terracotta-coloured aluminium: a gesture of harmony to the historic pavilions, but a slightly surprising colour choice for such a streamlined form. The massing of the architecture responds to the contours of the site's topography, as the circulation route from the lobby-level courtyard passes beneath the curvilinear modern wing to the guest villas, which fan out down the hillside to the beaches below. Although the promenade from 19th century eclectic classicism through clean-edged formal modernism to the secluded paradise of the guest rooms tells a very Singaporean tale – and one that can only be experienced by very few – the refined and deferential nature of the contemporary architecture stands in stark contrast to the 'oblivious to the context' banality of much recent development on Sentosa Island.

ion orchard

orchard road
completed 2009
architect – benoy
with rsp architects

Due to their ephemeral nature, one is always reluctant to include shopping malls in architectural books, as their shelf life is inevitably so short (as with restaurants, nightclubs and the like) that entries will be nostalgic within a year or two of publication. However, the Ion Orchard development is so significant from an urban planning perspective, as it sits in the heart of the Orchard Road shopping strip above the Orchard MRT Station, that to disregard it would be neglectful. The intersection of Orchard, Scotts and Paterson Roads is possibly the city's most significant, and it would be nice to believe that one day it will be treated as such: as a Times Square, a Piccadilly Circus, a Ginza or a Nanjing-Lu. But the Ion Orchard, for all its peacock dazzle, fails to engage with the public realm, and, as a consequence of its integration with the MRT station, it actually sucks people away from the street and into a vast network of subterranean shopping canyons: astonishingly, Ion's street-front forecourt is now almost always deserted. Pedestrians can no longer cross the road from the Ion corner, they are forced to descend into and negotiate crowded warrens of shops and food outlets to emerge ten minutes later on the other side. This may be perceived as commercially rational – part of the Orchard shopping experience – and helpful for traffic flow, but it sure kills the street life. A complete rethink of the intersection may be timely, particularly in terms of the vehicular traffic, most of which could surely be diverted elsewhere.

The Ion Orchard development comprises two parts: a retail podium containing eight levels of shops, and a fifty-six storey residential tower, which is placed to the rear. The podium features Asia's largest media façade, wrapping over a sinuous skin beneath a transparent canopy, which is supported by two large and rather ungainly metal 'trees'. The apartment tower is discreet and elegant, although caught in that default setting of adapting a cold-climate template to a tropical city by simply adding a series of balconies to a sealed surface. However, criticism of Ion Orchard's architectural intentions is possibly churlish, as the retail podium was intentionally designed as a landmark of the fleeting kind, and as a seductive curvaceous advertising hoarding for the mall's high-end boutiques.

The open tracts of land occupying what would appear to be large and valuable sites within the city form a distinctive feature of Singapore's urban landscape, and one that looks rather puzzling to the visitor. These unused spaces – covered with grass, used as pedestrian shortcuts, and claimed by Indian workers for weekend games of cricket – have been set aside by the government for future development. The policy has ensured a rational (on the most part) and orderly evolution of the built environment, but the barren fields form quite an impediment to the natural flow of urban activity, and diminish the scale and impact of the city itself. The URA (Urban Redevelopment Authority) has attempted to remediate the problem by establishing what they describe as 'interim parks' where 'public spaces can be enhanced'. One of these interim parks occupies an elongated stretch of land running between Penang Road and the eastern end of the 'Golden Mile' itself: Orchard Road. The central and western sectors of the land are covered with trees, providing a pleasant though noticeably underused environment, whilst the eastern sector has (for the interim, one assumes) been named Dhoby Ghaut Green, and adjoins the Dhoby Ghaut MRT Station. A spiraling structure, accessed from the east and west, contains a small sunken amphitheatre within an inclined enclosure of 'woven' aluminium strips and timber battens. The form of the structure, especially when viewed through a newly landscaped grove of trees to the west, is most beguiling, as the aluminium strips ripple and shimmer in the sunlight: the surface does resemble that of a rattan basket, as intended by the architect. The public space has been enhanced, as it provided the opportunity for a sculpted, expressive and constraint-free piece of architecture, but as to whether it supplies any tangible amenity for the city remains problematic, as an interim park sited between two very busy roads may forever be out of sight and out of mind.

dhoby ghaut green
penang road
completed 2009
architect – scda

CARLTON
SMU

orchard central

orchard road
completed 2009
architect – dp architects

Billed as Singapore's first vertical shopping mall, the twelve levels can be reached by a set of four external escalators, forty-eight internal escalators and twelve glass elevators, which is a lot of vertical transportation. The mall has a relatively long street frontage of 160 metres, so the horizontal circulation routes are also quite extensive. The internal arrangement of boutiques and food outlets appears to have been determined by the complexity of the circulation, which has constrained the pre-requisite connectivity and ambience of a successful shopping centre. As the complex is placed on a narrow site, the height of the interior volume feels rather intimidating, as if the mall should really be an office block, where such hierarchical stacking is accepted, if not welcomed. The building sits on a prominent site at the eastern end of the southern wall of buildings on Orchard Road, and its twelve-storey elevation acts as the gateway to the Orchard Road area from the city. The crowning façade of Orchard Central forms an unmistakable landmark, with a faceted agglomeration of triangular metal screens that shimmers in the sun as it rises above the tree canopy: a sprightly sight that represents a move away (and possibly a generational shift) from the prevailing sobriety of the Orchard Road shopping strip.

resorts world sentosa

artillery avenue
completed 2010
architect – michael graves
with dp architects

Michael Graves originally came to prominence as a member of the New York Five, also known as the Whites, who designed a series of houses between the late 1960s and mid 1970s that fervently espoused a return to the purist principles of early modernism. Then, in the words of Charles Jencks, "... he moved away from a Late-Modern abstract style toward a more accessible language with historicist references." In other words, he embraced Post-Modernism, and he was to become one of the movement's brightest stars, designing two of its most memorable buildings, the Humana Building in Louisville, Kentucky, and the Portland Building, Portland, Oregon (both 1982). Post-Modernism was not to take up many pages in the histories of architecture – it did not linger longer than the 1980s – but it appears that Michael Graves did not move away for a second time in his career. According to the architect, Resorts World emphasises the local tropical character, and (he says) it does not look like it could be anywhere in the world. Upon viewing, it might be possible to suggest that an integrated resort whose design themes veer from Versailles to Las Vegas, and from Rio to Siena by way of Universal Studios, does not emphasise the local tropical character so much as obliterate it. But the phantasmagoria is worth a quick look, if only to contemplate the curve of an architectural trajectory that began with purist principles and ended at Resorts World, where the largest hotel is named Hotel Michael.

marina bay sands
bayfront avenue
completed 2010
architect – moshe safdie
with aedas

When a work of architecture becomes the image or the symbol of a city, subsequent analysis of the project in a formal or functional sense is possibly less relevant, and certainly less interesting, than that of its popular significance. Marina Bay Sands is not perceived as a piece of architecture so much as an object that now defines Singapore (and the corollary is... for better or for worse), but one is curious as to why. The Bilbao effect (or the Sydney Opera House effect, or the Colossus of Rhodes effect) is engrained in contemporary geo-political myth making, but when one is tip-toeing along that fine line between architecture as art and architecture as statement, one can feel rather nonplussed by the relative successes and failures of iconic architecture, much as one is always puzzled by the fickle nature of popular taste. Both the Guggenheim Museum Bilbao and the Sydney Opera House were immediately acknowledged as putative landmarks in the course of architectural development – the innovations (and the time-honoured tweaking of the form/function ratio) were clear – but one suspects that Marina Bay Sands will slip through the net of accredited history, as its most dynamic attributes essentially comprise a monumental reworking of 1950s structural expressionism. The fantastically exaggerated profile and the parabolic tensions of Marina Bay Sands cast the complex in the role of a bombastic grandchild of Eero Saarinen's Dulles Airport Terminal (1958-63), which is no bad thing in itself, but the architecture can hardly compare in terms of precision and technical audacity with that of Saarinen (or indeed Jørn Utzon, who designed the Sydney Opera House in 1957).

The casino/shopping/convention/hotel complex has quickly established itself in a collective consciousness (far beyond Singapore) because its form is so unusually enigmatic, not to say eccentric, for such a conspicuous structure. All the metaphors and explanations offered for its shape and configuration are unconvincing – surfboard and waves, Stonehenge, ancient tablets – and perplexingly non-Singaporean, so it may perhaps be deduced that the design intention (or process) was simply an exercise in monumental abstraction and a reversion to primal form-making. However, the abstraction and the heroic forms appear to have been compromised during construction (the low-lying buildings are surprisingly rudimentary), the extravagant usage of air-conditioning in the atria signals another 1950s revival, and the entire complex neglects to engage with its waterfront location (apart from the quirky cupped hand of the ArtScience Museum): all of which means little to the tourists, the gamblers and the image-builders. The architecture's endurance as an 'icon' is probably unlikely, as one suspects that the impact has been one of happenstance – Singapore had been searching for a symbol, and it got one of sorts – and it must be observed that an architecturally revisionist casino complex is not the type of edifice by which civilisations (or cities) choose to be remembered.

school of the arts

bras basah road
completed 2010
architect – woha

If the School of the Arts appears inordinately large for a secondary school, it is due to the nature of its structure, whereby the elements (the classrooms and circulation routes) are set up as a massive space-frame. Variously scaled voids are overlooked by galleries of classrooms and linked by breezeways throughout a structure that is never enclosed: the circulation is never blocked, and the wind is continuously channeled through all the spaces. The structure is thus a massive exercise in passive ventilation – it is a wind machine – and the school requires little in the way of air conditioning, as the breezes are constant. The two functions of the building – the upper teaching levels and the lower-level performance spaces – are clearly legible from the street as a bipartite layering: a base of heavy masonry and shadowed voids sits below three vine-clad one-room-thick classroom blocks, which rise as prongs above the trees on the southern elevation. The passageways and spaces of the lower levels are deliberately unsettling (in comparison to the breezy brightness of the classrooms above) and rather claustrophobic, walled with rough-ribbed shards of tawny off-form concrete. The six levels of classrooms were conceived of as a 'blank canvas' by the architects – they would supply little in terms of decoration in the communal areas, leaving that to the students – so the surfaces and details appear austere and utilitarian in comparison with the verdant walls of tumbling vines.

The School of the Arts is one of the most resolved of WOHA's prototypes for genuinely sustainable architecture: where forms and elements are manipulated at a grand scale to create shaded naturally-ventilated spaces, both public and private. And, as an early 21st century rarity, the building stands as an uncompromising monumental expression of its structural function.

tokio marine centre

mccallum street
completed 2010
architect – chan sau yan associates

Apart from the few blocks immediately south of Singapore River, the city's CBD is remarkably dreary, with medium-rise office towers walling the three main arteries – Shenton Way, Robinson Road and Cecil Street – without offering anything distinctive. As so much of Singapore's commercial and civic activity is decentralised, the CBD is not particularly interesting in itself: it is pretty much confined to corporate office blocks and it feels surprising small in scale. The Tokio Marine Centre, regional headquarters for an insurance company, is possibly the first memorable downtown office block built for some time, and its proximity to the much-loved AXA Life Building (1975, James Ferrie & Partners) is most serendipitous. Chan Sau Yan has practiced architecture in Singapore and Malaysia since 1964, and has always been highly regarded for his houses and condominiums, but, with the exception of the Hotel Maya in Kuala Lumpur (1997), his practice has not been called upon to design large-scale public or commercial buildings, which would appear to have been an opportunity lost.

The Tokio Marine Centre, on a street corner with three clearly visible elevations, is distinguished by columns of off-form concrete, which pass across each other as they rise up the façades. The architect cites inspiration from a 'clump of bamboo' – which attains rigidity through natural criss-crossing – and the external placement of the columns enabled completely open floor-space, partially shaded by the columns themselves and by the outward flaring of the floor plates as the tower ascends. The building's muscular elemental proportions are dexterously composed and arranged, providing a much needed counterpoint to the timid, two-dimensional, appearance of the curtain-wall towers currently shooting up as an extension of the CBD on the reclaimed lands south of Marina Bay.

helix bridge

bayfront avenue
completed 2010
architect – cox architecture
with architects 61

This curving footbridge is a breathtakingly beautiful structure, comprised of two spirals of tubular stainless steel wrapping through each other in a three-dimensional curve, thus inspiring the inevitable allusions to the delineation of the DNA molecule. The bridge connects the massive Marina Bay Sands complex with the northern foreshore of the bay, and continues the promenade of the eastern and southern shores. Canopies of steel mesh and laminated glass are fitted within the tubes to provide shade and shelter, with cantilevered viewing pods protruding from the concave eastern curve of the bridge to provide the prerequisite photo viewpoints for the Singapore skyline to the west. The steelwork is beautifully detailed, and the elegant composition and clarity of form recalls the 1980s buildings of Philip Cox (the founding director of Cox Architecture), such as the Sydney Exhibition Centre and the Sydney Football Stadium: structures that displayed a sureness of touch and an unwavering conviction that the original concept was strong enough to see the project through without modification. As with the Helix Bridge, those buildings occupied that most compelling of grey areas, the zone where architecture and engineering overlap, and it cannot be a coincidence that Arup were the engineers for both the bridge and the earlier Australian projects. However, the siting of the bridge is rather puzzling to say the least: its convex curve is shoved up against an undistinguished concrete road bridge, so that the Helix Bridge cannot be seen in isolation, thus diminishing both the aesthetic value of such a graceful object and its usefulness as a Singaporean landmark. One can only hope that at some point in the future the road bridge will be deemed surplus to requirements, and demolished forthwith.

SOLARIS

The second building completed in the southern Fusionopolis precinct of the one-north technology-centric business park (Kisho Kurokawa's tripartite Fusionopolis tower was built a year earlier), Solaris is presently cast adrift in a sea of flattened construction sites, a temporary context that suits its nautical appearance. A continuous landscaped spiral ramp wends its way around the perimeter of the structure on a trail – over a kilometre long – from the parkland at the north to roof gardens at the top, so the building has a restless elevational profile, with layers of green sandwiched between the office floors. The white steel cladding is similar to that used by Ken Yeang on the National Library (2005), and responds sinuously to the undulations of the plan and the layering of the façades. A large atrium with a glass-louvred roof opens up the core of the building to allow daylight to penetrate the office floors from the interior and to establish natural ventilation through the structure. The three-metre-wide 'green' ramp was conceived of as a linear park with continuous vegetation: a ribbon of eco-structure wrapped around the building, thus providing sustainable natural cooling and shading. The plants are irrigated by rainwater harvested from the building itself. Solaris is a masterful achievement by the grand man of eco-design, but one wishes that the building wasn't hidden in a 'science-hub' office park, where it will only preach to the converted.

solaris

fusionopolis walk
completed 2010
architect – t.r. hamzar & yeang
with cpg consultants

Not so much a hospital as a sanitorium (deriving from the Latin *sanare*, to heal), which implies that a building should be restorative, and indeed, uplifting. Unless one is a proud new father, a visit to a hospital is generally a thoroughly depressing occasion, but entering the Khoo Teck Puat Hospital in suburban Yishun (far to the north of the island) is an unexpectedly delightful experience. The hospital is a park, or so it appears, with layers of plants cascading over four levels to a broad courtyard filled with trees. The courtyard runs the full length of the complex, between two blocks of wards, clinics and surgeries on a dogleg plan, which opens out to Yishun Pond at the north, thus funneling breezes from the pond through the hospital. A variety of ventilation and shading devices are utilised, with every elevation defined by arrays of screens, louvres, overhangs and planter boxes, so that fresh air is available as required within the wards. The courtyard is set below the street entry level, so the creation of new ground planes is integral to the architecture, and the scale of the complex is difficult to determine, as the massing of the architectural elements has been subverted by the layers of greenery, the internal tree canopy and the bridges between the two blocks. The formal architecture may have been obscured, but the circulation is easy to comprehend, as the complex has really been set up as a self-contained garden city. As so many hospitals have grown incrementally as soulless functional accretions, or as factories for health-care, one must celebrate a return to the restorative ideals clearly established by Alvar Aalto's Paimio Tuberculosis Sanitorium (1933), where the architecture prioritised the provision of fresh air and sunshine, and an adjacency to nature.

khoo teck puat hospital
yishun central
completed 2010
architect – rmjm hillier with cpg consultants

punggol promenade

punggol road
completed 2011
architect – look architects

Punggol Point is a location with many memories, associations and connotations for Singaporeans. Punggol (Malay for 'throwing sticks at branches of trees to knock the fruit to the ground') was a farming district until the relentless march of the new towns reached the edges of the island a decade ago, and Punggol Point – separated from the Punggol new town by a tract of tidal swampland – looks across the one-kilometre wide Strait of Johor to Malaysia and the docks of Johor Bahru. The beach at Punggol Point is inscribed in the Singaporean collective memory as the site of a 1942 massacre, when the Japanese invaders shot 400 Chinese civilians. A shallow curving beach of white sand – much like that of Changi Point (eight kilometres to the east) where sixty-six Chinese were executed – edges a delicate and gently beautiful littoral landscape oblivious to the horrors visited upon it. The Punggol Promenade, a sensitive and deferential timber walkway placed lightly on the grasses above the beach, acknowledges the significance of the location with an austere material palette, which, in the words of the architects, "... carries undertones of sobriety in tribute to a sliver of history." The profile of the cantilevered lookout platform recalls imagery of the World War II Pacific Theatre (battleships steaming into conflict at Midway) and serves as both a rusted and abstracted memorial for those aware of the site's poignancy, and a maritime observation platform. The timber planks of the walkway have already weathered and faded, whilst the angular steel railings mounted on black concrete plinths are as uncompromising in appearance as the lookout platform. The promenade must also be seen in the context of a newly discovered appreciation of Singapore's much overlooked natural beauty: the Strait of Johor is a wonderful stretch of water, much undervalued in the context of the modern city, and this narrow strip of parkland provides a non-intrusive opportunity to re-engage with the island's natural enclosure.

space asia hub

bencoolen street
completed 2011
architect – woha

Strategies for preserving historic buildings and precincts in the face of relentless demands for modernisation are many-fold and, it must be said, most have been adjudged unsatisfactory. The gratuitous retention of a historic façade, behind which resides a standard-issue modern building, is the most common and expedient solution to heritage considerations. But paying such lip service adds nothing to the aesthetic and functional qualities of a city, which is undeniably better served by the adaptation of its existing building stock. Respectful, coherent alterations and 'improvements' to historic structures are possibly the most successful and uplifting of solutions. As Singapore moves beyond the instinctive compulsion to build something completely new and purely self-referential every time the opportunity arises, sensitive and thoughtful maintenance of the city's existing architectural fabric will be fundamental to the city's growth.

The showrooms for Space Furniture occupy two conserved 19th century buildings – a villa and a shophouse – linked by a new orthogonal L-shaped block clad with reflective glass. The timber floors and ceilings, and exposed brickwork of the existing structures were retained, so that the deceptively large interior of the shophouse feels like a warehouse, or an art gallery for furniture. The exterior of the contemporary building is conspicuous by its absence, it serves only to mirror the decorated façade of the villa and the trees of Bencoolen Street, whilst its internal spaces have an intangible, stylistically elusive presence, as they contrive to mesh the disparate levels and elements of the entire showroom into a navigable network of discrete furniture displays. By drawing attention to the restored buildings, the unequivocal modernist intervention has, paradoxically, enhanced the civic virtues of the existing architecture. As Singapore becomes inexorably more chic, similar boutique developments will flourish, and the city will continually regenerate itself by respecting, utilising, and improving upon what it already has.

my waterway@punggol
punggol walk
completed 2011
architect – surbana

Singapore's urban expansion, which began in the late 1960s as new towns spread out from the city centre in the south, paid little attention to the landscape. The program of modernisation had other priorities, but the urban degradation and environmental despoliation that usually accompany the rapaciousness of civilisation can be quickly overcome in Singapore: as the landscape was easy to build upon, so is it easy to remediate. Not many significant landforms had been sacrificed for HDB blocks, re-vegetation is not a complex process, and the flat, often swampy plains can be reconfigured and newly beautified. As a newly matured Singapore's thoughts turned to self-sufficiency, sustainability and lifestyle quality, the creation (or re-creation) of parks and waterways on the unused flatlands surrounding the new towns would restore a tropical habitat, provide unprecedented local amenity, and play a role within the island-wide water retention scheme. My Waterway@ Punggol connects two reservoirs, which were created by damming the Sungei Serangoon and Sungei Punggol, with a new river (in place of a planned pipeline) that runs east-west to the north of the Punggol new town. The landscaping surrounding the meandering watercourse of the western sector is now complete (the eastern waterway is straight), and the real joys are to be had from the reinstatement of a natural environment: terraces of green grass tumble down the slopes from the surviving rainforest of the northern marshlands, with walkways extending over the river as *kelong* style platforms or footbridges. Other man-made interventions, such as concrete feature walls and traffic bridges, are unfortunately very heavy-handed, but the success and the value of the project is not dependent so much upon the ephemeral details as it is upon the big picture: Singapore is creating landscape, rather than destroying it.

marina bay financial centre

marina boulevard
completed 2012
architect – kohn pedersen fox with dca architects and architects 61

In terms of the Singapore downtown cityscape, the last decade of the 20th century was distinguished by the Marina Centre and Suntec City developments, north of Marina Bay, where a selection of North American architects contrived to transform an equatorial city into Houston or Minneapolis. Orthogonal office blocks and hotels – clad uniformly in grey stone or aluminium and containing vast air-conditioned atria – tower above wide boulevards and public spaces that have never been peopled (it's too hot). The architecture and planning were obviously inappropriate for a tropical city, although understandable in terms of Singapore's image-building at the time. Move on twenty years and it's happened again, directly across the water, only the towers are now sealed in blue glass, and the redundant boulevards have been replaced by an underground connection system and shopping complex, instantly recognisable to the citizens of a large provincial American city. As at Marina Centre, Singaporean street-life – one of the city's most cherished and charming cultural assets – has been vapourised, sucked underground and thoroughly air-conditioned. The architecture is not bad per sé, but it is almost perversely neutral: anonymity taken to the point of invisibility. The site was a fantastic opportunity, as it linked the heterogenous skyline of the existing CBD to the willfully eccentric forms of the Marina Bay Sands complex, but the only thing that can be said about the completed project is that nobody has really noticed it. The ensemble of four towers does, however, constitute a rather unlikely tropical tribute to the American downtown skylines of the early 1980s, when clusters of reflective glass towers huddled together to keep themselves warm.

international cruise terminal

marina coastal drive
completed 2012
architect – bermello ajamil and partners with rsp architects

The existing terminal – at Keppel Harbour, between Telok Blangah and Sentosa Island – had become unable to cope with the ever-increasing size of visiting cruise ships, due to the constrictions of the dead-end channel. A new site, with deep water and room to manouevre, was selected on the edge of the vast tract of reclaimed land southeast of the city. With its dynamic roof forms and full-speed-ahead geometry, the new terminal is particularly striking from a distance and from sea: a Futurist vision of a majestic liner charting a course through the hundreds of container ships at anchor off Singapore's port. Upon closer inspection however, the external construction and the internal spaces appear quite prosaic and rudimentary, which – despite acknowledgment of the corrosive maritime context – is rather disappointing in terms of the presumed sophistication of the international cruise ship lifestyle, where one might expect at least a hint of opulence. As the terminal is presently three kilometres (and a taxi trip through construction sites) away from Singapore itself, the jet-set ambience may have been placed on hold for a few years.

bishan – ang mo kio park

ang mo kio avenue 1
completed 2012
landscape architect – atelier dreiseitl

Despite the extraordinary amount of rainfall the island receives, Singapore retains little water, it has no natural aquifers, and the last fifty years of urban development has exacerbated the run-off process, with much of the rainfall heading out to sea through a network of concrete canals built in the 1960s and 1970s to alleviate flash-flooding. In 2006, the PUB (Public Utilities Board) implemented a plan that would enable complete water-supply self-sufficiency by 2061 (Malaysia currently supplies forty percent of Singapore's water). Basically, Singapore is to become one large reservoir, by closing off all its rivers to the sea, by recycling and storing its water through pumping stations and existing reservoirs, and by creating new reservoirs where the rivers had been dammed at their mouths (most notably at the newly designated Marina Bay in the city centre).

The Kallang River is Singapore's longest river, and the first three kilometres of its path flows through Bishan – Ang Mo Kio Park, which separates the new towns of Bishan and Ang Mo Kio. Until recently, the park was nothing special: swampy and effectively unusable, as are many wide-open spaces for much of the day in Singapore. But the precinct was seen as an opportunity to accomplish something special within the framework of the PUB master plan, and Atelier Dreiseitl proposed a return to nature, whereby the canal would be torn apart and replaced by a meandering creek, which would perform as a natural cleansing mechanism for the water and reduce the speed of its flow. The canal was demolished (the smashed concrete fragments were then used as construction material), the slopes of the riverbanks were cambered to contain floodwaters and covered by plant cuttings, which were laid down as a carpet of twigs that would sprout into life during the wet season. A cleansing 'biotope' – a micro-environment or natural habitat that filters and regenerates water through layers of plants, roots, sediments and earth – was installed in the upper half of the park, with a children's water playground included within the cycle of the watercourse.

The completely revitalised park is astonishingly beautiful, in what might be seen as a return to the 'picturesque' 19th century landscaping of Frederick Law Olmsted in the USA. The park is an idealised micro-environment, deliberately employing viewpoints that gaze over romantic vistas created by the contours of the landforms, the existing treescape, the banks of reeds and grasses, the placement of rock formations, and most overtly by the course of the river itself. It is a pastoral landscape, and its 'back to nature' intentions have been reinforced by nature itself, as the park has been quickly colonised by wildlife and wildflowers.

gardens by the bay

marina gardens drive
completed 2012
architect – Grant Associates and Wilkinson Eyre

The grand plan for Gardens by the Bay was announced in 2005 and trumpeted by Prime Minister Lee Hsien Loong as Singapore's 'premier urban outdoor recreation space' and a 'national icon'. The gardens would comprise three precincts – Bay East, Bay Central and Bay South – facing each other across the Y-shape of Marina Bay, of which one, Bay South, has been completed. Bay South, which is currently referred to as Gardens by the Bay, features two large waterfront conservatories and eighteen man-made 'supertrees' (between twenty-five and fifty metres in height), set in fifty-four hectares of gardens. The site adjoins the Marina Bay Sands complex, and the architectural forms of the conservatories harmonise neatly (and presumably coincidentally) with those of the neighbouring mega-structure: both sets of architects had the templates for expressed modernist structure – as per Pier Luigi Nervi and Eero Saarinen – close to hand. The swelling (shell-like) arrays of hoops that cage the conservatories are satisfyingly spritely, if formally unadventurous: something of a missed opportunity when viewed next to the unsettling and visually compelling proportions of Marina Bay Sands. The purple painted 'supertrees' are far more interesting, and hilariously contradictory in terms of their function, as they were essentially designed to perform as trees: the irony implicit in the arboreal installation demands that urban landscape requires a degree of evaluation from the public. Mammoth artificial trees are the stuff of sci-fi movies set on damaged planets, so can the 'supertrees' be viewed as prototypes for damaged cities, or are we simply being entertained?

apartments and condominiums

the loft apartments

nassim hill
completed 2002
architect – w architects

Mok Wei Wei (who formed W Architects after working with William Lim for many years) had become immersed in an architectural evaluation of what he refers to as his 'Chineseness' and, by extension, the Chinese heritage of Singapore. The Loft Apartments reflect this preoccupation, which came about as a reaction to the avowedly representational work of his previous practice, and specifically draws graceful abstracted connections with Chinese landscape painting and the gardens of Suzhou. He was clearly, but not provocatively, refusing to 'tropicalise' his architecture in terms of its appearance, although he was, of course, mindful to maintain sun shading and ventilation. His Chinese (East Asian rather than Southeast Asian) inflections do suggest quite convincingly that tropical architecture can be elegant and delicate in appearance, as the massing of the apartment blocks is veiled by façades of permeable glass, vine-clad trellises, and slender projecting blade walls. Five four-storey blocks of apartments enclose a large triangular courtyard, which contains a lap pool, a shallow children's pool, and a wonderfully seductive landscape, which is fundamental to the 'mood' of the condominium. Mok has transplanted the subtleties and the ambience of the revered Chinese gardens: his forms are modern and orthogonal, but they are softened and abstracted by gently drooping willow trees, by the reflections from the pools, and by the asymmetrical arrangement of the landscaping elements and the apartment blocks. The condominium is a highly private self-contained environment, shielded (as with other of Mok's contemporaneous projects) by solid external walls on each of the apartment blocks.

lincoln modern

20 lincoln road
completed 2003
architect – scda

SCDA, founded by Chan Soo Khian in 1995, quickly established a formidable reputation for modernist (and self-described 'neo-tropical') domestic architecture, but has now become a practice most synonymous with elegant apartment towers in Singapore and Kuala Lumpur. The towers demonstrate an innate sense of formal composition and harmony, with a subtle and sensitive external delineation of the interior program, and the slender Lincoln Modern was the first to display the architects' inclinations. The eastern façade, a discreet but sharply detailed curtain wall with anodised aluminium cladding, reveals that the apartment block comprises two separate towers, split on this elevation by two orange blade walls, which enclose the fire stairs and lifts. The composition is subtle yet assertive, a sign of things to come, with the mundane servicing requirements of a high-rise tower acknowledged as components of the elevation, rather than as elements to be disguised. The apartments within each tower utilised a crossover section (referring back to the Russian Constructivist innovations of the 1920s), thus providing a double height living space with a single storey bedroom, a configuration quite clearly designed for a certain (child-free) demographic. Each apartment interlocks with another, so that pairs of apartments are stacked upon each other: two blocks in the northern tower and one in the southern tower. This arrangement is clearly expressed on both façades, as the interlocking units appear to clamber up the building. The sheer elevations descend abruptly into water – a lap pool on the east and a shallow reflection pool on the west – where SCDA display the refined and abstracted landscaping (replete with judiciously placed large pots) that has come to characterise their work.

1 moulmein rise
completed 2003
architect – woha

Although some notable apartment towers had been built in the 1970s, such as the Futura Apartments (1976, by Timothy Seow) and the Pearl Bank Apartments (1976, by Archurban), the condominium block had, by the end of the century, become so formulaic and blatantly developer-dictated that architectural innovation played a marginal role at best. The Asian economic crisis of 1997 shook things up to the extent that developers were prepared to seek architectural input: as potential buyers were now picking and choosing, the developers had to find new blandishments, and architectural quality was now a preferred option. A limited competition in 2000 for a condominium development at the base of a small hill in the Novena area was won by WOHA, a small practice known for a clutch of houses, which had received much local praise. WOHA, who had never previously designed a high-rise, took the opportunity to shake up the entrenched formula, which was, as they observed, "... floor plans stacked on top of each other, so that the form of a high-rise has nothing to with the plan." The other entrants to the competition had proposed typical medium-rise blocks with four units per floor, whilst WOHA proposed a slender tower with only two apartments on each floor, reasoning that the increase in construction price would be more than offset by the high-rise amenity, especially the views of the city and the sea to the south: a persuasive argument, and readily accepted by the developer. The strategy must have been successful, as Singapore's more well-heeled districts, and Novena in particular, are now distinguished by an archiscape of towers with similar building envelopes.

The tower has an elegantly silvered appearance, with the southern façade presenting itself to the city as a seemingly random pattern of windows and screens on its eastern half, juxtaposed with a stack of strip windows and overhangs on the west. The northern façade is clad by a skin of perforated aluminium, which conceals the services and fire stairs. WOHA have further developed their ideas for tropical high-rise living with a series of apartments throughout Asia, but (although they have always retained the one-room-thick apartment plan and the double-layered skin) they have never designed another slender stand-alone tower.

trevose 12
trevose crescent
completed 2003
architect – bedmar & shi

The work of Ernesto Bedmar, an Argentinian who set up practice in 1986, is both innovative and reflexive: he has been indisputably influential, many times over, as he has responded to more than twenty years of social, economic and material evolution within his affluent constituency. His earliest houses were personalised adaptations of a Balinese style, and he can be credited with introducing this romantic typology to the suburbs of Singapore, one which rapidly captured the imagination of local homeowners and architects. He was quick to add other ingredients to the mix, and he set the pace through the 1990s with a succession of villas that employed a combination of robust masonry with exotic timber detailing and idyllic landscaping. As the new decade began, he abandoned the crafted languor in favour of an abstraction of form, characterised by monumental walls, open volumes, formal landscaping and crisp elegant detailing, although his commitment to tropically attuned architecture remained intact. The Trevose 12 condominium was a clear demonstration of this reconciliation between abstracted modernist form and tropical indulgence: twelve virtually identical townhouses are set above the street on an existing natural platform, with formal rectangular elevations. The townhouses appear tall and narrow – the individual sites are only ten metres wide – but the height and length of each volume is crucial. The apartments are only six metres wide but twenty-four metres long, and rise over four levels from the car park. A four-metre wide garden and lap pool are placed between the apartments and a sheer stone party wall, so the fully glazed volume of each townhouse is completely private, yet filled with light on all four levels. The (four by one) proportions are similar to those of the traditional Singaporean shophouse, which provided light and ventilation through a central lightwell, so it might be observed that Bedmar has deconstructed and opened up the shophouse.

the arris apartments
yan kit road
completed 2003
architect – w architects

A companion piece to the Paterson Edge apartments, completed four years earlier, the Arris Apartments were built at a time when Mok Wei Wei (the principal of W Architects) was intent upon establishing a distinctive ethereal form of modernist architecture. Both the Arris Apartments and Paterson Edge are difficult to read from the street, as the elevations are diaphanous and delicate, with sheer glass curtain walls and stiffly projecting sunshades contriving an illusion of infinity, and eluding objective perception. The roadside trees are appropriated as integral part of the elevational composition, both in substance and in reflection, and are also used as an additional form of sun shading. The Arris comprises two blocks on a triangular plan, which tapers to a slender southern elevation capped by a cantilevered swimming pool. The two blocks are split by the entrance lobby, and in complete contrast to the pellucid eastern elevation, the western walls are built from thick and heavy masonry in order to shield the apartments from the afternoon sun.

THRE3

three three robin
completed 2005
architect – w architects

A desire on the part of the developer to maximise the views from within a highly congested precinct of apartment blocks determined that the orientation of Three Three Robin would run north-south, thus exposing the tower to the morning and afternoon sun. The western elevation was clad with sliding panels of timber louvres, whilst the eastern elevation was nakedly modern, with white-painted shelves shielding the glazed apartments from the sun. The impact of the mass, which thrusts itself northward in contradiction to its neighbours, is reduced by a large void carved out beneath its northern edge and by a grouping of three smaller low-rise blocks on the eastern side, which are glimpsed over the swimming pool. The overtly dualistic appearance of the building is quite dramatic, as both façades have a heroic presence, although it must be conceded that the duality is only created by a set of timber screens. The quality and the precision of the detailing and the rigorous composition of the elevations are appreciable from a distance, where the apartment block can be observed as yet another variation upon the modernist prototypical slab-forms of Le Corbusier's Pavilion Suisse (1933, Paris) and Unité d'Habitation (1952, Marseille).

blvd residences

cuscaden walk
completed 2005
architect – scda

A twin-apartment tower development that displayed a new level of architectural quality and finesse at the top end of Singapore's residential marketplace: in other words, the architecture significantly updated the image of a preferred lifestyle. The BLVD Residences followed two other apartment projects (Lincoln Modern and The Ladyhill) by SCDA for SC Global, a property development group that has distinguished itself by using Singaporean architects in preference to those who may or may not completely understand the requisite methodologies for tropical construction. The form of BLVD was determined by the shape of the site and by its position at the top of a small rise between Orchard and Grange Roads. Two thirty-six storey towers, each with a rectangular plan, are connected by sky bridges, and the massing is calibrated to take advantage of the winds and the views: the two parallel towers are stepped across the site in order not to impede each other's views and to facilitate air-movement between the blocks. The manipulation of vertical massing and the consequent composition of materials have come to characterise SCDA's high-rise architecture, and the northern façade is a particularly tasteful assemblage of surfaces and elements: the fire stairs are screened by a perforated aluminium skin, adjoining a double-glazed curtain wall braced by green glass fins, which is edged by cantilevered concrete balconies. By virtue of their articulation, the colours, the materials and the forms appear seductive and cool, and subtle yet expressive.

robertson blue

robertson quay
completed 2006
architect – chan sau yan associates

Built to conform to an envelope control plan (stipulating a maximum height of ten storeys, a common lot boundary and the retention of sixteen metres of existing warehouse) the Robertson Blue apartments overlook the Singapore River with a fully transparent façade and full-length balconies cantilevered from the load-bearing cross walls. This delicate glazed elevation contrasts with the off-form concrete rear façade, which has a strong formal expression, and, although it currently looks onto a vacant block of land, is cognisant of the imminent built reality of its location. One might have thought that off-form concrete would be much more widely used throughout Singapore, as its low maintenance and insulation properties are most appropriate to the local climate, but these considerations are presumably outweighed by a residual aesthetic condemnation within a certain marketplace (private apartments and condominiums) that identifies the use of concrete with low-cost housing. Chan Sau Yan Associates have chosen to use off-form concrete in several subsequent apartment projects – notably Park Seven in Kuala Lumpur (2008) and Mont Timah in Singapore (2011) – as have Kerry Hill Architects in the nearby Martin No. 38 (2011), so the breezes of common sense may be blowing through the serried ranks of Singapore's white-painted 'air-condominiums'.

newton suites

newton road
completed 2007
architect – woha

As the result of a small, quite rational, but fundamental, shift in the architects' thinking, the Newton Suites apartment tower looked profoundly different to WOHA's previous buildings. The practice had become very well known in a short period of time for programmatically resolved and clinically detailed projects – a series of houses, the Church of St Mary of the Angels and the 1 Moulmein Rise apartment block – but the architects were unwilling to float along at that level, remunerative as it may have been, and were agitating to grapple with broader issues and solve bigger problems. Newton Suites stands as a symbol of that creative restlessness: for all its dexterity and structural innovation, it appears to have been deconstructed and reconstructed several times over. The antithesis of sleek (although it was finely detailed), the thirty-six storey tower is clad with a bristling carapace of black steel sun-screens and seemingly smothered with greenery. A green wall of the *thunbergia* vine stretches one hundred metres from the basement to the roof, and so intrigued other architects that the building achieved an instant and unexpected global notoriety (now, of course, the strategy has become commonplace). The car park podium is completely covered by *thunbergia*, a series of cantilevered communal sky gardens extend from the lift lobbies, and the greenery component of the site was increased by 130 per cent, which was (reputedly, as formal ratings were not then in place) an unprecedented achievement. The apartments, each with a protruding balcony, were placed four to a floor and separated by large breezeways. The architecture was a vigorous and assertive display of WOHA's desire to implement a sustainable tropical architecture that would rely upon structural and spatial manipulation, and the extensive use of greenery, to create ventilation and shade on a grand scale.

pan pacific serviced suites

somerset road
completed 2008
architect – cpg consultants

Most notable for its unusual curved profile, this sixteen-storey apartment building was created by the recalibration of an existing office block in the heart of the Orchard Road district. The vogue-ish 'live-work-play' model was used for each apartment, anticipating the effortlessly compartmentalised lifestyle of the global traveler (who was, presumably, moving upmarket from the humdrum reality of the 'work-sleep' model), so the suites can be easily reconfigured from a single open space to twin rooms, and from an office to a dining room to a formal reception area. A full-height atrium – lined with open-air corridors – rises between the two blocks of apartments, naturally ventilated from the open ends of the building, thus obviating the need for massive public air-conditioning (an incongruity that remains fashionable in even the most recent Singapore hotels). The façades are double glazed, with bay windows (containing LED lightboxes in their ledges) running as strips across the two frontal elevations. The curved base of the apartment block sits sixteen metres above a swimming pool area on the podium roof, so that the side elevations appear to derive from the cross-section of a huge round-bottomed alabastron vase held upright by a set of slender columns.

botanika

holland road
completed 2009
architect – scda

A beautifully detailed and overtly contextual condominium, Botanika contains only twenty-seven apartments and nestles within a cluster of rain trees edging a dense forest to the north. The elements and materials take their cues from the tropical landscape: the timber-clad massing of the structure is effectively camouflaged by projecting layers of screens, and the light filters through to the apartments as it would in the forest. Full-height windows provide sweeping views into the tree canopy, whilst louvres, trellises and protruding balconies shield the apartments from the sun. The plan of the apartment block cuts back to an acute triangle at both ends, which creates a dynamic profile within the treescape: a thrusting organically-attuned gesture atypical of contemporary Singaporean architecture. Sightings of environmentally responsive domestic architecture, particularly an architecture that mimics the appearance of the landscape, have been notably rare in modern Singapore. This circumstance is possibly a consequence of the emergence of a society that was preoccupied with financial and social progress and an assertion of self-determination: an attitude that was (possibly sub-consciously) opposed to a perpetuation of what might have been construed as a colonial, or vernacular, approach to living in the tropics.

It would be hard to overestimate the significance of this project in terms of Singapore's recent history. HDB apartment blocks (named after the Housing and Development Board) have been key to the economic growth and social cohesion so desperately sought after the horrors of World War II, the breakup of the British Empire, and the country's subsequent struggle for survival. Housing had become a critical problem: in the late 1940s, Singapore's slums were adjudged to be amongst the worst in the world, and things had only slightly improved by the late 1950s. The newly elected PAP Party passed the Housing and Development Act in 1960, which initiated a low-cost government-built housing program. High-rise high-density apartment blocks then began to march (and continue to march) inexorably across Singapore: they are generally owned by their occupants, and it is estimated that ninety percent of the city's residents live in what are always referred to as HDBs. The HDB estates, and the new towns they inhabit, are a source of much pride and have become a symbol of Singapore's success: far from looking down upon the occupants of housing estates, most Singaporeans aspire to own a dream HDB.

The HDB towers prioritised affordability over architectural value, and the Duxton Plain Housing Competition of 2001 sought to redress a perceived imbalance between a condominium lifestyle and that of the HDBs: a perception that arose as Singapore's citizens became more affluent and lifestyle conscious. 227 architectural practices from thirty-two countries entered the competition for a high density HDB project on slightly elevated plot of land in the Tanjong Pagar district, just south of the city centre. ARC Studio, a relatively unknown local practice, were surprise winners with a scheme that was inarguably spectacular, ingenious, and (to use that dreaded adjective) futuristic. Seven fifty-storey towers were linked, high in the sky, by broad public bridges (referred to as sky gardens) on two levels, and the towers were placed on a curving plan that actually forms a question mark. Such undulating plans were characteristic of post-war low-rise European housing schemes – such as Park Hill in Sheffield, the Byker Wall in Newcastle-Upon-Tyne, and Émile Aillaud's Pantin-les-Courtillières housing in France – but these estates formed continuous unbroken concrete ribbons, they were walls, whilst the Pinnacle@Duxton is conspicuously permeable with great gaps between the towers. Permeability – separating the elements of a structure to encourage air movement – has always been essential to vernacular (pre air-conditioning) tropical architecture, and the return to such a basic principle can almost be taken for granted in the 21st century. The discreetly random façade pattern, which resulted from the choices of each resident from a selection of bay windows, balconies and planter boxes, was a particularly effective way of breaking down the scale and the potential anonymity of such large towers. The massive project (it contains 1848 apartments) presents a distinctive profile when viewed from the city streets and – due to its twisted elongated plan and its proximity to other towers – it is almost impossible to see in its entirety, but the building is always there, an HDB as a mega-structure looming above the old lanes of Tanjong Pagar. As opposed to its 20th century European precedents, it is an urban (rather than suburban) scheme, and it is occasionally hard to believe that something this audacious, and so emblematic of Singaporean identity, actually got built.

pinnacle@duxton
cantonment road
completed 2009
architect – arc studio
with rsp architects

skypark

st thomas walk
completed 2009
architect – mkpl architects

Every apartment – two per floor – in this narrow tower was designed as a 'house in the sky', with a double-height living room overlooking a large garden terrace. The interlocking layers of the southern elevation clearly articulate the modular configurations of the twenty-eight floors of apartments, which are raised four floors above the ground level swimming pool and amenities. The two-storey apartments are each accessed from a lift lobby through private gardens, and the immediate view through the living area to the balcony gardens does encourage one to believe that the apartment is a landed house. The architecture is not formalistically remarkable, but it does point the way for intelligent sustainable tropical apartment design, which stimulates natural ventilation and firmly establishes greenery as an integral part of city living, even when one's house is on the twentieth floor.

belle vue residences

oxley walk
completed 2010
architect – toyo ito with p&t consultants

This secluded and exclusive condominium has been assiduously promoted as an integration between the natural and built environments, which, to quote Toyo Ito, "... is more than a bond between humans and nature, it also brings the serenity of nature into one's life." Comprising 176 apartments within a five-storey compound, the condominium has a relaxed ambience facilitated by a continuous sinuous water feature, and by gentle landscaping that screens the serried ranks of the apartment blocks. This ambience, the integration of architecture and nature, is something of a conjuring trick as the project is very densely built, and it might be observed that the integration of nature was absolutely essential if privacy was to be obtained. Be that as it may, the condominium is quite beautiful, it is an urban oasis, and with timber-clad bridges linking timber-clad apartment blocks through groves of slender trees, the 'tree-branch typology' alluded to by the architects may be sufficiently beguiling as to beget as much serenity as you could hope for (or pay for) in the heart of the city.

reflections at keppel bay

keppel bay view
completed 2011
architect – daniel libeskind
with dca architects

A prosaic description of this apartment project – "six twisting and tapering glass towers with chamfered roofs arranged in three pairs, which are linked by sky bridges" – is pretty much unnecessary, as are the adjectives – "breathless, mind-blowing and awe-inspiring" – used to convey the presumed impressions of an architectural naïf upon initial viewing. The ensemble is spectacular and compositionally delightful, a bravura exercise in stalagmite form-making from an internationally acknowledged master of the genre, but, as sour and cynical tutors in the later years of one's architectural course are wont to ask... 'What does it mean?' Flamboyant form-making, architecture as architecture, may be regarded as an end in itself, and many highly revered practitioners throughout history would propose that such a position is ineluctably the only thing that they can rely upon: I design, therefore I am. But the erection of six self-referential glass-clad towers, set upon the waterfront within a secluded residential compound in a tropical city, does beg a few questions. On the one hand, the height and density of the development are mindful of the shortage of land in a highly populated small island, and the fantastic geometry of the towers provides Singapore with another architectural icon to show off to the world. On the other hand, one might ask how the architecture responds to its tropical – and specifically to its Singaporean – context in any discernable fashion. Any formalistic engagement with its location is hard to deduce, apart from the 'curves look nautical' metaphor beloved by all seaside real estate franchises, but the development's environmental response is possibly of more concern, especially in terms of the message that it delivers: huge towers clad completely in glass are acceptable if the architecture is terrific. One might contend that such architecture is not acceptable, never mind sustainable, when it is washed up on the shores of an island one degree north of the equator, no matter what the eco-data ratings might tell us. Singapore is not New York, nor is it Dubai, and as we hurtle into the 21st century, one might suggest that the transportation of such a monumental building type from one climatic zone to another requires a little less wow and a little more now. However, as a fantastic vision (in a Land of Oz kind of way), Reflections at Keppel is something to behold, even though (as one final quibble) it is rather difficult to behold, as the exclusive condominium is located well away from the city and best viewed from a yacht.

the marq
paterson hill
completed 2011
architect – scda

The Marq represents a subtle evolution in SCDA's apartment design, with a larger scale implementation of the interlocking sections first seen at Lincoln Modern (2003), a refinement of the interplay between sun-screening devices and of the clear external articulation of interior configuration, and an extension of a formal precise landscaping from gardens to grounds. Two twenty-four storey towers sit at right angles to each other on either side of a water garden, with the more architectonically assertive tower – distinguished by an array of cantilevered swimming pools on either side of every second floor – placed further to the north. The apartments in this tower have four bedrooms stacked on two levels, the living and dining areas occupy a double-height space that leads out to the pool terraces, and a light and breezy internal environment is facilitated by extensive operable glazing.

Shade is provided by horizontal extruded aluminium sun-screens, which delineate the internal structure on the curtain-wall façade and set up a contrapuntal rhythm with the vertical fins that screen the shafts of services. The towers are placed to the south of a large walled site with manicured lawns, a discreet clubhouse and an unexpectedly ceremonial *porte-cochère*, all of which contribute to an atmosphere of resort-style exclusivity. The formal glazed elegance of tropical modernism – which, until recently, was seen as having a much wider application – has become increasingly confined to the apartment block and condominium, whilst new-found imperatives for sustainable tropical architecture are determining more elemental structural solutions elsewhere in the 21st century city. It will be interesting to see whether the twain shall ever meet at the top end of the marketplace.

martin no. 38

martin road
completed 2011
architect – kerry hill architects

Located in a relatively neglected pocket of low-lying land contained with a loop of the Singapore River, this fifteen storey apartment block takes advantage of the lack of context and neighbouring architectural distinction to create its own identity, and in doing so, suggests a new direction for local urban style. The architectural language is industrial and uncompromising, but never flirts with grunge. This is a designer industrial, loft-style development – SoHo comes to Singapore – for a city that never had that kind of urban fabric: Singapore's historic inner-city working environment was low-rise, thus unretainable in terms of land value, apart from the go-downs (warehouses) on the river. The massing is elegantly poised, with an off-form concrete slab encased on its southern elevation by a steel-framed cage of sliding aluminium louvred panels, so that the building appears as twin blocks of concrete and metal. Calibrated for a tropical climate, the detailing and the proportions are refined and elegant, and each of the ninety-one apartments has a flexible layout, whereby walls and doors can be configured to suit the occupant. The residential tower is set back behind a two-storey podium block, which continues the rectilinear metal and concrete geometry. The form and structure nimbly resolve any questions of climatic appropriateness, but the building's 'Singaporean-ness' is less assured, as the formal austerity of its appearance is specifically identifiable as that of recent urban regeneration projects in the post-industrial inner-city wastelands of many Western cities.

mont timah
bukit way
completed 2011
architect – chan sau yan associates

Located at the end of a cul-de-sac and surrounded by the monkey-filled jungle of the Bukit Timah nature reserve, the context of Mont Timah was very special, and the architectural response – in off-form concrete – was assertive and boldly articulated, yet harmonious and willing to integrate with the organic profusion. Two rows of three-storey blocks flank a swimming pool and communal garden on a site sloping down from the entry, with each block containing four apartments on a pinwheel (or *sauwastika*) plan. The volumes are stepped and staggered, and the concrete walls are occasionally stained a charcoal grey, so that the agglomeration appears willfully haphazard: an effect heightened by the luxuriant and slightly unkempt landscaping of the gardens. The composition of the condominium and the choice of materials reflect an artful intent, one of attempting to tame the wilderness at the edge of the jungle whilst acknowledging that it cannot be done. A constant tension between the dynamic and the static, and the abstract and the organic, prevails throughout the compound as a particularised version of a tropical truth, where human intervention can only be seen as ephemeral. The extent to which this truth may no longer hold is evidenced by the placement of huge picture windows in each apartment, from where the residents can observe the wilderness (tamed or otherwise) on their own terms. Mont Timah is a notably clever and scenographic piece of architecture, which engages and reciprocates with both its external context and its internal landscape to create an idealised tropical environment, just where the city meets the jungle.

houses

kheam hock house

completed 2002
architect – aamer architects

Set above the street on a natural plinth, replete with lap-pool, the Kheam Hock House appears disarmingly transparent and elegant, quite at odds with the hermetic massing and introverted landscaping of its neighbours in an affluent precinct off Bukit Timah Road. The focal point of the elevated set piece is the double-height living room (with a small mezzanine), where a graceful and beautifully detailed shell of timber battens wraps around the top half of a glazed cube. This living room adjoins an intricately composed entry vestibule and staircase, which utilises a robust material palette of crafted teak joinery and roughly hewn stone, complemented by glass and slender steel fittings. The contrast between massive and ethereal is adroitly manipulated throughout what might be described as an architecture of appropriate tropical modernism. Too many contemporaneous Singaporean houses adapted a northern European architecture to the local context with a gratuitous tweak here and a gratuitous tweak there, but the Kheam Hock House responds indulgently, and with great panache, to the delights of its location.

andrew road house
completed 2002
architect – scda

This house, or residential compound, can be seen as the forerunner for many of SCDA's resort and condominium projects. An overtly formalised (thus relentlessly orthogonal) sequence of spaces and circulation routes implies that every object on the site – whether it be a water feature, a living pavilion, a sculpture or a tree – is an artefact in its right, and worthy of contemplation and respect. Of course, this strategy requires a careful selection or creation of objects, and subsequent judicious emplacement: a process that has been semantically defined over the last decade (particularly in commentary upon tropical resorts) as the 'choreography of space', an undeniably romantic, but rather vapid appellation that implies something unprecedented and mercurial. An geometric manicured landscape that defers to its artefacts and leads the visitor directly to preferred viewing points is not exactly a recent phenomenon, but the adroit arrangement of the architectural elements within the composition has undeniable advantages in a tropical context.

Roofs, overhangs, screens and water are all utilised to encourage cooling breezes and provide plentiful shade on a gently sloping site. A large internal courtyard with a swimming pool is enclosed by three flat-roofed pavilions and accessed from the street by a raised stone pathway, which passes through a striated stone-clad wall above a reflection pool. A transparent 'reception' pavilion sits to the north of the pool, between a lower level eastern pavilion screened with metallic mesh, and an elongated timber-clad volume – screened by another striated stone wall – to the west. The palette of materials – timber, stone, mesh and steel – is integral to the harmony of the design, which artfully contrives an ambience of languor through the precision of its composition.

A robust off-form concrete shell creates a formidable armature for an introspective house, which takes up most of a relatively small site hemmed in by its neighbours. The gardens are placed within the S-plan of the house, with a spacious living room and an outdoor dining area looking across to each other over a water courtyard containing a frangipani tree. The interior spaces of the house are beautifully crafted, employing a seductive material palette of roughly-hewn stone blocks, teak flooring and joinery, and etched glass, The bathrooms are an exercise in tactile interior décor: the bathroom for the master bedroom is encased within glass and off-form concrete walls beneath a glass roof, whilst the ground floor powder room – with a floor of black polished pebbles – is open to the sky. An external stone-clad winding staircase leads to a roof garden with another frangipani placed in a reflecting pool. The architecture is sedate and assured: so assured, in fact, that a visitor is oblivious to the site's contextual constraints and limitations.

sunset vale house

completed 2005
architect – wow architects

white house park house

completed 2005
architect – hb design

Aligned longitudinally over a site inflected by the convex curve of the road, two conspicuously different pavilions are linked as one house by a small water garden. A bedroom block is seemingly hermetically sealed in pale turquoise frosted glass, whilst the living pavilion is transparent and extroverted, defined by a monumental rusted steel (cor-ten) blade wall to the north and by massive projecting eaves. The distinction between the pavilions, which appear to all intents and purposes to be separate houses, is part of a constant process of contrast throughout the interior and the exterior. Every edge is sharp and every surface is pristine, as a clinical high-tech sensibility has been diligently applied to a domestic setting. Materials and form are always seen in opposition, but due to a synchronisation of proportions and scale, the overall composition is balanced and harmonious: the abundance of detail appears logical within such a rigorously controlled environment. By way of a further contrast, the house is overlooked by a forested hillside and surrounded by mature trees, so the precision of the structure is always seen against an unruly tropical backdrop.

cable road black & white house

completed 2008
architect – chan sau yan associates

Black and White houses, a very localised type of bungalow, were constructed (mainly in the 1920s) as accommodation for colonial administrators, and are now regarded with a nostalgia somewhat at odds with Singapore's recently acquired predilection for all things modern, and its tacit lack of interest in the colonial era. The Black and White houses are fondly regarded, however, because they are so identifiably Singaporean, because they look so striking (spacious bungalows with a Tudor twist), and because they respond so well to the climate. The Cable Road house was in poor condition: the entire upper floor needed to be replaced as the timber had deteriorated badly, and the ground floor walls required reinforcement. The original driveway was relocated from the south to the north, so that the *porte cochère* became a verandah, open to the gardens. A swimming pool with timber decking and a cabana were placed to the east of the bungalow, and most significantly, a new pavilion was erected to the north. This new wing, which contains bedrooms on the second floor, above the garage and kitchen, is linked seamlessly to the bungalow by a new internal staircase made of folded plate steel with timber treads. The extension is deferential, and by employing a clean-edged modernist language, it avoids the stylistic confusion created by formal integration, however subtle.

26 cable road house

completed 2008
architect – ip:li architects

To genuinely step back in time is rather unusual in local architecture, although lip service has been paid to the traditions of the shophouse, the *kampung* house and the colonial bungalow: especially in terms of enclosure and domestic hierarchy. The forms of landed houses built in contemporary Singapore have never strayed far from a typology that can only be described, upon dispassionate observation, as northern European. As Singaporeans grew wealthy and, with great relief, embraced a materialist culture that they had only too recently presumed had been denied forever, they commissioned houses that would proudly demonstrate the new-found status: as they purchased Ferraris, so would they build the architectural equivalent. Singapore emerged as a putative First World country in the early 1990s, at which time the sleek European sports cars and the sleek European houses came to define the new affluence. The non-architectural houses (locally disparaged as monster houses) paid no discernable attention to the tropical climate, as air-conditioning and heavy curtains obviated the need for any further intervention, whilst the better architect-designed houses mediated European modernism (learned as gospel at university) with various methods of sun-screening and cross-ventilation to produce an architecture that has, with subtle twists, been categorised as Tropical Modernism (and which is now perceived throughout Southeast Asia as a Singaporean type). But, there was an alternative, one grasped by Yip Yuen Hong of ip:li Architects, who was fundamentally preoccupied with Singapore's traditional lifestyle and heritage, and the possibilities that could be offered by contemporary interpretations of a local history.

The house at 26 Cable Road is set well back on a densely vegetated wedge-shaped site that widens from the entry. A two-storey pavilion, flanked by a lap pool, is surrounded by a sand garden with gently raked paths wending through the trees, so that views of the house are inevitably framed or obscured by foliage. The architecture does not seek out attention: it is recessive and porous, with a dark-painted timber and steel framework enclosing wide-open spaces. The ground floor living area is one great breezy shaded room, open to the pool on one side and a sunken pebbled-garden on the other, whilst the upper storey bedrooms are arranged around a central space that should really be termed a verandah. The framework is beautifully detailed, with slender columns – often arrayed as pairs on a single footing – establishing an elegant formality within the languid dimly-lit landscape. One hesitates before using the word 'romantic' in terms of architecture, but as Yip articulates his principles in a manner that is both sentimental and idealistic, one cannot shy way from observing that his architecture constitutes a romantic manifestation of a tropical ideal and a local culture: one that is quietly insistent that Singapore should be Singapore.

windcatcher house

completed 2008
architect – k2ld

The commanding, one might even say formidable, site for the Windcatcher House determined an architectural response that was, by turns, both assertive and deferential. On the crest of a small hill overlooking the Botanic Gardens, a stand of large *tembusu* trees did not provide a screen of foliage so much as an organic monument with which architecture could never compete. The heavy stone walls and sturdy volumes of the house complement the massive dimensions of the *tembusu* trees, whilst the repetition of slender columns and timber screens suggests an undergrowth within a forest. Delineation between interior and exterior space at ground level is unclear, as the transitional areas – the verandahs – surrounding the central swimming pool form an continuation of the formal living areas, most notably the double-height dining room. Two bedroom volumes were placed to the north and south of the pool: the shorter northern entrance block is solid, with an external wall of roughly-hewn granite chunks, whilst the southern pavilion comprises a second floor bedroom wing (clad with recycled *tembusu*) supported by angled black steel poles in the void below. The second-floor circulation route passes through a gallery above the dining and living room. The enclosure of the compound is difficult to discern, as vistas of the distant tree-clad landscape have been borrowed, to be viewed between gaps in the stone walls and through the open space below the southern bedroom wing. The work of K2LD Architects is underpinned by an evasion of formality, by an abstraction of materials and elements, and by a volumetric connectivity, which are subtly attuned to the potential of a specific context: both in terms of engaging with that context and as an opportunity to create an architectural set piece.

The Cluny House is one of a series designed by Guz Wilkinson in the heavily-treed landscape of Singapore's most exclusive residential areas, where the environment is uniquely conducive to the provision of beautiful tropical houses, ones which embrace their exotic context without equivocation. Wilkinson's early Singapore houses (designed in the late 1990s) were firmly indebted to the Arts and Crafts movement, whose thick walls, projecting eaves and free-flowing spaces were appropriate for protection from the heat, which wasn't a great breakthrough (Frank Brewer had established an Arts and Crafts style with houses built between the 1920s and 1950s), but it denoted a 'swimming against the tide of modernism' approach at odds with his peer group. He was then to update the ideas and principles of these houses to a point where he could almost intuitively arrange every element of the architecture and landscape within a three-dimensional composition that responded to the context of its site.

The secluded plot of land for the Cluny House was tucked away at the end of a cul-de-sac, and Wilkinson placed two pavilions on an L-shaped plan at the perimeter. The two-storey house overlooks a wonderful water garden, comprising a large fishpond with an 'archipelago' of tree-filled islands, which appears to merge with a lap pool enclosed within a glass rim. The pavilions are festooned with greenery (bouganvillea and phyllanthus), which spills out from the second floor to camouflage the massing of the house. A verandah, below a roof garden, projects into the water garden with a vine-draped trellis extending across the lap pool. The house and the landscape possess a multiplicity of viewpoints, but every vista is internalised, confined within the boundaries of the site: the compound is completely self-referential, a world within a world.

cluny house
completed 2008
architect – guz architects

fish house

completed 2009
architect – guz architects

Sentosa Cove, which unabashedly proclaims itself to be 'the world's most desirable address', is a residential enclave (or gated community for the wealthy) on the eastern tip of Sentosa Island, four kilometres south of the city. The estate is largely built upon reclaimed land and comprises precincts for condominiums and private villas, which either face out to the sea or the harbour, or internally to a network of artificial canals. Notwithstanding the enclave's global desirability, the plots for the villas are very small, so the owners and their architects have maximised the amount of house on each site. The houses are frantically overbuilt, squashed together like passengers on a budget airline, and attempt to outdo each other's architectural narcissicism (although, due to the prescribed building envelope and the minimal manicured landscape, the streetscape is surprisingly homogenous).

Guz Wilkinson, with the encouragement of his client, took what might appear to be the only sensible response to this context: he underbuilt. The site for the Fish House had a magnificent view, looking out to small palm-treed islands over the sea, and – wedged between the blank wall of its neighbour and a small sub-station – it was very secluded. Two small pavilions were linked on the northern edge of the site by an open walkway and a set of stairs, and the sea-side living pavilion is enclosed by a U-shaped swimming pool. The ground floor of this pavilion is an open verandah and the second floor is completely glazed, so that virtually unimpeded sea views can be had from the street-side bedroom pavilion. A basement entertainment area, below the verandah, looks into the swimming pool through a panoramic acrylic window. Both the second floor master bedroom and living room were open-plan with curved timber ceilings and soffits, giving the house a decidedly nautical air. Photovoltaic cells line the roof of the bedroom pavilion, and a green lawn covers the living room: a backyard on the roof. The house and pool combine to create a wonderful micro-environment, one that calibrates the constraints of the Sentosa Cove plot size and building guidelines to enhance the pleasures of its location.

apartment house

completed 2009
architect – formwerkz

The family compound could be considered as an architectural type in itself, especially in Southeast Asia, where the fine line between a *kampung* and a domestic residence has often been little more than a row of flowering plants or a well-swept path. Many Singaporeans have attained a new affluence and a new taste in material pleasures, but the social structures and familial ties remain well in place. The architectural response to the requirements of a family compound in modern Singapore has been more than edifying, as so many local architects implicitly understand the hierarchies within an extended family, and where the lines between private and communal should be drawn. If nothing else, modernist architecture was a great leveler, and is thus well attuned to the relatively egalitarian nature of a family compound. The forms and materials – and the modernist language – used throughout the Apartment House do not signal the prioritisation of any individual within a multi-generational family, as the heterogenous assemblage of elements obviates any sense of scale. The swimming pool and its decks are very much the focus of the house, forming a central public space updated from the sand garden or paved courtyard of yore. Privacy and transparency are both possible, as the timber screens and the circulation routes can be calibrated to suit the occasion, and the internal layout and fixtures were planned to be flexible and replaceable, so that the compound can be reconfigured as the constituency of the family changes over the years.

enclosed open house

completed 2009

architect – wallflower

Until the massive land reclamations of the late 1960s, the Mountbatten Road area had led a laidback existence as a seaside escape for the wealthy, who built villas and the occasional mansion on the flatlands near the beach. The villas, generally single-storey and raised above the ground as the area was prone to flooding, were set back in generous gardens and were formalised though unpretentious variations upon the *kampung* style of house then prevalent in suburban Singapore (and still common in Malaysia). After the land reclamation, which extended the shoreline by a minimum of 600 metres out to sea, the villas were left high and dry, separated from the sea by walls of apartment blocks, an eight-lane expressway and the thin strip of East Coast Park. Slowly, but inevitably, the blocks of land were sold off and the villas began disappearing. As Singapore's desire for real estate development has accelerated so rapidly in the 21st century, the point has been reached where few villas remain, as the land value has overwhelmed the worth of a small functional house, but (to an extent) the laidback ambience lingers. The site for the Enclosed Open House was previously occupied by a villa and garden, within a cul-de-sac of villas and gardens (gone or going) and the new house maintains the scale of the Mountbatten Road precinct, as the two-storey villa is set back twenty-five metres from the road, with discreet arrays of vertical timber louvres as the only visible elevations. A rectangular grassed courtyard sits between two long pavilions, which are connected by walkways at both ends, and the bedrooms are all placed on the second floor so that the ground floor comprises one 40-metre open space: flowing from the entrance foyer, over a swimming pool, and through the two transparent living areas and the grassed courtyard. The air movement is constant and refreshing, due to a process of horizontal convection induced by the fluctuating temperatures of the various indoor and outdoor environments. The escape-from-the-city feeling, which characterised the neighbourhood for so long, has been sustained by an architecture that prioritised space and breeze, and that refrained from overbuilding.

lien villas

completed 2009
architect – the lien villas collective

The Lien Villas Collective comprised six local architectural practices – K2LD, Ministry of Design, Zarch Collaboratives, Terre, Metropolitan Office Experimental, and PODesign – who were brought together to each design a villa on the sloping garden beneath a conserved colonial bungalow. The owner of the site originally approached Ko Shiou Hee of K2LD Architects (who had previously designed two houses across the road) to draw up a master plan for the placement of six villas, preferably not separated by large boundary walls, as they were intended for rental. Ko suggested that six architects should be selected to design six villas – citing the precedents of Nexus World Housing (Fukuoka, Japan, 1991) and the Commune by the Great Wall (China, 2002) – in a manner that both respected and contrasted with the historic bungalow. The master plan (carried out in conjunction with Tierra Design) was defined by an axis that bisected the length of the site, descending from the bungalow to the northern boundary. The subdivision of the land ensured that the individual plot sizes and shapes were so dissimilar that homogeneity of design would be out of the question.

The northernmost villa, the 8-Box House, was designed by PODesign (the architectural component of Tierra Design) as a stacked and twisted collection of eight white-painted cubic volumes with sloping roofs. The interior circulation reflected this three-dimensional interlocking with rooms that connected directly with each

8-box house : podesign (right), screen house : k2ld (opposite above), cubic house : zarch collaboratives (opposite below)

other and with the garden. The adjoining Cubic House, by Zarch Collaboratives, was the most lively and restless of the villas, an amalgamation of forms and materials that suggest that the architect was designing several houses simultaneously and decided to integrate them, to form a medley. The *promenade architecturale* through the house is quite extraordinary: one moves from bamboo gardens to transparent glazed living areas and red brick courtyards, and through hermetic enclosures walled with off-form concrete to the structural climax of the external 'tea-room', a jagged cage of black tubular steel. The Screen House, by K2LD, is less idiosyncratic and can be readily identified as a contemporary Singapore house: a strategy that possibly suited Ko Shiou Hee in his role as orchestrator within the collective. A two-storey block, screened by battens from the western sun, forms

raw house : metropolitan office experimental (below), patriarch house : terre design studio (opposite above), zigzag house : ministry of design (opposite below)

an orthogonal backdrop to the embrace of an ovate entertainment pavilion by a curvaceous swimming pool.

At the top of the hill, the existing bungalow was restored and extended by Terre Design Studio as the Patriarch House, a 'meeting house' for the family that owns the site. The extension comprised a white-painted concrete two-storey pavilion, connected to the bungalow by an enclosed footbridge. The interior of the bungalow was completely refurbished to house a beautifully crafted combination of period furniture, contemporary retro cabinetwork and ornate metal screens. The Raw House, by Metropolitan Office Experimental, comprised two rectangular volumes stacked at right angles to each other. A massive living room, fully glazed on the north and east, looks over the roofs and trees of the other villas, whilst the western façade forms a solid mass to block out the sight and sound of a nearby arterial road. The *yin* of the Cubic House sits opposite the *yang* of the Zigzag House by Ministry of Design, which makes a virtue of the unambiguous expression of a single determining idea. The project's only single storey villa snakes across the

lowest point on the site, with an almost totally transparent façade revealing an open interior, whose rooms are defined by the zigs and the zags of the plan. The roof is covered with bright green artificial turf.

The Lien Villas project was probably a one-off, as patrons with sufficient wealth to facilitate such an undertaking are few and far between, and as such, it will provide a fascinating snapshot of Singaporean architecture and Singaporean society at the beginning of the 21st century. A communal ideal can only exist for the already affluent in a materialistic society where houses don't come cheap, but one might observe that it has been forever thus and hope that the compound can be retained *in perpetuam* as an architectural and social exhibit.

cove way house

sentosa cove
completed 2009
architect – bedmar & shi

This hermetic, self-referential house – as they all are at Sentosa Cove, due to the small plot size and the extreme proximity of the adjoining villas – comprises two blocks, separated by a triple-height atrium with a dining room at the basement level. The street-side bedroom block is faced with a forbidding stone wall that frames a vertical array of folding timber shutters, and is capped by an attic level entertainment space with a folding timber ceiling. The rear pavilion, looking out to a canal over a raised lap pool, has been treated as an outdoor living space – a double-height verandah – below a screen of slender battens and a glass roof. This seven-metre high volume is enclosed by three walls of folding timber shutters, which can be opened out to the view and to catch the breezes, or used to screen the living room from its neighbours. On a sunny day, the striated pattern created by the battens and the angled shutters is quite bewitching. A mezzanine level looks over the double-height space to the canal, and is linked to the bedroom block by glass bridges over the central void, which is walled on one side by teak shelving. The rear pavilion is a uniquely wonderful space, ostensibly an ideal inside/outside environment for tropical living, but the monumental scale of the bi-fold shutters (and presumably the effort required to operate them) declaims the problems set by tightly controlled residential estates, where the procurement of precious space becomes the architectural priority.

It is tempting to read too much into this house, as it does appear as a beacon of common sense in a landscape of architectural hubris, so one must bear in mind that Guz Wilkinson's strategy was one of remediation rather than innovation. The client required a house that, in the architect's opinion, was too large for its site, and as such, ran counter to everything that he stood for. There was little he could do to reduce the bulk of the massing, so he broke the blocks apart to create a full-height internal void, he layered the levels as external terraces, and he covered the entire house with lawn, shrubs and trees. The internal courtyard – featuring a twisting overlapping set of stairs – extends through the length of the house from the entry to the canal frontage. This courtyard and the permeable façade optimise natural ventilation in all directions, and the atrium serves as a space for the process of convection (or thermal lift), which constantly draws cooler air up from the ground floor to be released at the top. As with all houses in gated communities for the wealthy, one is reticent to claim a victory for sustainability (the context of over-building is simply too contradictory) but one assumes that the architect's ecological strategies – which created this most 'green' of houses – can be acknowledged in terms of the house itself.

meera house
sentosa cove
completed 2010
architect – guz architects

golden box house
completed 2010
architect – k2ld

The Tanglin area is one of Singapore's most gorgeous precincts, a secluded heavily-treed and permanently shaded neighbourhood on the eastern fringe of the British colonial army barracks (recently reinvented as a chic shopping and restaurant enclave). The Golden Box House gleams in the dappled daylight as a sparkling presence within an all-pervading landscape of greenery: a precious object sheathed by a diaphanous shimmering skin. The client for the house had, curiously, but unequivocally, requested a house that would resemble a 'transparent shopping mall' and would maximise the permissible building envelope (no retreat into the rainforest here), which – although something of a double-edged sword – appealed to the architects as an opportunity to design a house that might disappear within its own gilded cloak. A screen of golden mesh is wrapped around the second floor of the house, and set well apart from the solid volume, much in the manner of a billboard or a hoarding, whilst the ground floor is glazed and transparent: an open-planned living space that the architect describes as 'un-private'. A cranked blonde-timber spiral staircase connects the living area with the basement entertainment room – containing a full-sized bowling alley – and the second-floor bedroom level. An aluminium-clad box on the roof contains a study, which opens out to shallow reflection pools and timber decking. The external detailing of the house is ornate, though not ostentatious: the patterned metalwork of the entry gates and the golden mesh hint at arabesque, which is possibly an appropriate allusion for a house where the massing has performed a disappearing act, veiled and obscured by iridescent layers and screens.

ninety 7 @ siglap road

completed 2010
architect – aamer architects

Not many Singaporean architects took much notice of the theories of 'folding' and 'wrapping' that flamed brightly in turn-of-the-century architectural thinking, and which were characterised most publicly in various works of Zaha Hadid. Fluidity of form ran counter to the prevailing preference for orthogonal modernity, especially in domestic architecture, and an enfolding skin seemed singularly inappropriate to a climate that insists upon structural permeability. The Kheam Hock House (2002) by Aamer Taher was demonstrably one of Singapore's most successful (orthogonal) tropical modern houses, but he followed that up with the Sundridge Park House (2004), which sheltered rectilinear massing with a great curving roof. This roof also performed as a wall on the eastern elevation, and although Taher was consciously looking back to the modernist forms of Oscar Niemeyer and Marcel Breuer, he was providing Singapore with a new contemporary 'type'. As great gaps were left between the orthogonal volumes and the sweeping roof, the Sundridge Park House was permeable: it couldn't help itself. The architect then took the next step, and designed a house that was both totally fluid and highly permeable. The Ninety 7 House is perched on the top of a small ridge, looking west to views of the city, and was perfectly sited to capture the hilltop breezes. The house has an L-shaped plan, with guest bedrooms on the ground floor, a dining room and living room on the second floor, and the master bedroom and family area on the top level. The dynamic forms of the roof/wall and the balconies overtly express the tropicality of the design – the acceleration of air movement and the munificent provision of shade – and it will be intriguing to observe what impact it will have upon local domestic architecture.

sarang house
completed 2011
architect – woha

The Sarang House, an elongated one-room-thick house placed at the northern perimeter of a family estate, can be seen as a master-planning exercise as much as an individual piece of domestic architecture. The extensive hilltop grounds of the compound contain existing houses set within a landscape of tall trees and rolling lawns, and the curved timber and metal screens of the southern elevation of the new house appear as an ethereal framing device within that context. A low wall separates the house from the gardens, but as all the bedrooms and living areas look over the family compound, the landscape is treated as a shared environment. The northern elevation comprises a set of monumental planar walls, which slide alongside each other to provide complete privacy whilst admitting daylight and providing airflow. The gently rusticated grey stone trimming of the white-painted walls establishes an air of crafted artlessness, which is continued with the joinery of the internal spaces and on the screens of the southern façade. It might be fanciful to think that the architects were intending to casually undermine the trophy house paradigm of finely wrought perfection, but it is quietly reassuring to note that some architects (and presumably their clients) can engage with the gentle arts of home-making as well as they can contribute to the valorisation of a desirable piece of land.

armadillo house

completed 2012
architect – formwerkz

The requirement to protect the occupants from continuous traffic noise – from an arterial road overpass and a slip road – created a house that looks, to all intents and purposes, like a freeway sound barrier. It is a boutique sound barrier though, with four overlapping walls of terracotta-coloured aluminium panels, which fold over the interior spaces to block the sound and vision of the traffic, and exposure to the western sun. Daylight enters and air flows through the gaps above and between the panels, and views are oriented to the north.

Environmental sustainability with minimal use of air-conditioning was achieved by placing the main living areas within a sunken and shaded internal courtyard, with a process of convection throughout the height of the house encouraged by the installation of mechanical fans on the roof. The elevation can thus be seen as a diagram of vertical 'stack' convection within a heat-shielding structure, whilst the overt protectiveness of the form (exaggerated by the homely silhouette of the party wall) serves as a visual riposte to rush-hour traffic.

3 lermit road house

completed 2012
architect – ip:li architects

Not so much a piece of architecture as an implementation of common sense, the additions imbued an undistinguished fifty-year old house with some dignity and some much-needed privacy. The existing house was set back from a seemingly insignificant, but constantly busy, road near the Botanic Gardens, and the volume of traffic had become such that the space between house and road could not be used. From the street, the addition looks like a house, as two large brick walls with an extravagantly cantilevered *porte cochère* appear to form a cubic volume, but the structure functions as a sound barrier and a massive enclosure for a newly created garden within. The existing house defers to its newly vegetated courtyard, the rustication of the brick walls and the off-form concrete framing, which will soon be festooned with creeping vines. The perforated walls function as an environmental screen, denoting an acknowledgment of the simple but effective breeze-block sun-screening devices employed in the local modernist architecture of the 1960s and 70s, and a tip of the hat to an architectural peer group in Malaysia and Indonesia who have espoused a return to hand-made craftsmanship.

The area now known as Joo Chiat was originally a large coconut plantation (owned by Chew Joo Chiat) and is renowned for its eclectically decorated rows of shophouses, built in the 1920s and early 1930s by the Peranakan community, the descendants of Southeast Asia's original Chinese settlers. 518 shophouses were gazetted for conservation by the URA in 1993, and a subsequent process of remediation has included some internal remodeling along with external cosmetic surgery. Joo Chiat might be euphemistically referred to as a mixed-use area, and whilst some of its precincts may flirt with the idea of gentrification, the neighbourhood at large retains an ambience unlike any other in the modern city.

The Lucky Bookstore, well known to generations of local schoolchildren, occupied the westernmost of three shophouses wider than others in their row, and its renovation took advantage of this unusual capaciousness to create three living areas that feel inordinately large for a shophouse. A narrow concrete backyard – shaded by trees from adjoining properties – extended north from the Lucky Bookstore, and the architect placed five modular blocks (almost cubic, with a length of 3.6 metres) as a garden house on a staggered plan. The stripping of the plaster inside the shophouse had revealed a rough red brickwork that simply had to be retained, and all thoughts of smooth plastering (for both old and new) were then banished. A small grassed area between the shophouse and the garden house preserves vistas from the adjoining laneway, with the dining area of the shophouse looking across to the open reading room of the garden house. A strategy of amplification, whereby a cramped shophouse was transformed into a massive volume, and of seclusion, with the insertion of a modular bunker beneath the trees, has created a grand yet introspective living space in the heart of a neighbourhood that has yet to be commodified.

lucky shophouse
completed 2012
architect – chang architects

winged house
completed 2012
architect – k2ld

A triangular site determined a V-shaped plan, whereby two blocks splayed out from the entrance to enclose a terraced lawn, protected by a large stand of mature trees. The section, rather than the plan or the elevation, became the point of interest, as the forms of the masses were teased apart in order to encourage ventilation, to provide an overwhelming sense of spaciousness, and to fill the house with daylight. Overlapping triangles form the *leitmotif* – the recurring visual theme throughout the house – with the shape and appearance of the roofs, ceilings, eaves, stairs, glazed elevations and roof gardens. Such a strong three-dimensional geometry resulted from the dissection of two trapeziums: firstly in order to place a floating roof above the bedrooms and balconies on the second floor, and secondly to install another, a roof above a roof. This filleting of the horizontal planes provided a set of expansive and elegant 'parasols', shielding the house and pool area from the tropical heat and monsoonal rain with an exhilarating play of external forms. A large living area beneath a roof garden transforms the V-plan into an A, and opens out to the lawn through glazed sliding doors, whilst the corridors and private rooms are constantly inflected by the exterior light conditions, as daylight filters through the splits between the roofs, the adjustable timber screens and the external plantings. The dynamic geometries and spreading layers – something of a return to the organic principles of a previous era – represent a break from the orthogonal rigidities of tropical modernism, which had held sway in domestic architecture for the previous decade. The house can thus be seen as a stimulating response to the exigencies of sustainable construction, as the formal and architectonic explorations had a demonstrably tropical resolution.

19 sunset place house
completed 2012
architect – ip:li architects

Built in the 1970s, the Sunset residential estate has a secluded and conventionally suburban ambience, which feels anomalous to contemporary Singapore. Other Southeast Asian cities, notably Kuala Lumpur, have large tracts of middle-class housing from this era, which retain a dignified period charm with bungalows that comprise variations upon a standard type, but Singapore's suburban spread was vertical (HDB apartments) rather than horizontal, although pockets of modular suburbia remain, as a kind of interim zone between the HDBs and the exclusive precincts of the landed gentry. The adaptation (to provide more space for the owners) of an existing 1970s house on Sunset Place preserved the internal 'project home' configuration of five split-levels and the quintessential historical décor, whilst encasing the existing brick-clad volume (and the new rooms) within a great concrete shell, as a house within a house. The project afforded the architect, Yip Yuen Hong, with an opportunity to indulge in a personal reverie with the essence of Singaporean living, away from the ephemeral pressures of high-end domestic architecture, where the extraordinary land values (created by the scarcity of available sites) have inspired an almost callous indifference to local context and memories. Yip did not wish to either improve upon or diminish the intrinsic 'worth' of the house or its location, and the shape of the new house is indeed that of a house (nothing more, nothing less) in the most elemental and generic fashion: a pitched roof and square windows. The unrelieved mass of off-form concrete appears antithetical to prevailing passive tropical construction, and although a thick casing of concrete is one way of keeping out the heat, the absence of external overhangs appears to be an almost willful re-alignment of thinking by an architect who was already well-known for his overtly-expressed sun-shading systems. But Yip was less concerned with expression than with particularised identity, and his idiosyncratic affection for (and his memories of) unpretentious Singaporean living was juxtaposed with an esoteric and impulsive desire for architectonic innovation.

under construction (2012)

the scotts tower
scotts road
architect – unstudio with ong & ong

images supplied by © unstudio

sky habitat
bishan street 15
architect – moshe safdie with
dca architects

d'leedon

leedon road
architect – zaha hadid architects
with rsp architects

images supplied by © capitaland

images supplied by © unstudio

singapore university of technology and design

upper changi road
architect – unstudio with dpa

skyville@dawson

dawson road

architect – woha

image supplied by © woha

skyterrace@dawson
dawson road
architect – scda

image supplied by © scda

national art gallery
st andrew's road
architect – studio milou
with cpg consultants

images courtesy of the national art gallery, singapore

nouvel 18
anderson road
architect – jean nouvel
with p&t consultants

images supplied by © ateliers jean nouvel

south beach
beach road
architect – foster and partners
with aedas

images supplied by © foster and partners

singapore sports hub

kallang
architect – dp architects
sports venue designer – arup
landscape designer – aecom

images supplied by © oaker

parkroyal on pickering

pickering street
architect – woha

oasia downtown
peck seah street
architect – woha

the interlace

alexandra and depot road
architect – office for metropolitan architecture with rsp architects

images supplied by © capitaland

index

CROWNE PLAZA
National Museum
of Singapore

Patrick Bingham-Hall is an architecture writer and photographer.

He is the author of recent monographs on WOHA Architects and Guz Architects, and a book on New Asia Pacific Houses.